IN AND OUT OF
LA LA LAND
MY JOURNEY TO BEAUTY AND CELEBRITY

Jeremy Mariage

Author's Note: Some names have been changed to
protect the privacy and identity of the individual.

Jeremy Mariage
jeremymariage@gmail.com

in and out of La La Land/Jeremy Mariage. -- 1st ed.
ISBN 978-0-692-12537-3

This book is dedicated to everyone who has a dream.
Just follow your inner self
and NEVER let anyone tell you,
"No, you can't."
Make things happen.
Do not wait for someone to knock on your door.
I have always said that everything happens for a reason.
Life always gives you two answers, "YES or NO."
Do not take rejection personally.
There's always going to be someone who will say,
"YES."
So, have a goal and go for it.
If you do not try, you will never know.
Trust me, I speak from experience here.
("When you wish upon a star...")

Contents

Malibu, California 2008

She had been on the phone trying to get a prescription delivered. She was frantic yet, as usual, always in control. She could not reach the doctor.

"I've been on hold all day. All day! Why won't my doctor call me back?"

I tried to reassure her.

"I'm sure he will call any minute. Don't worry. You know doctors; they take forever to call back."

"What is it for?" I asked.

"It's for my immune system, I really need it today," she answered. "The nurse is due tomorrow, so it has to arrive today."

The next morning, I waited for her to come down for breakfast. The housekeeper told me that she had not seen her yet and was probably still upstairs in her bedroom. I had some toast and watched TV in the downstairs guest bedroom, always mine when I stayed at her house.

Around lunchtime, I went to walk her dog. When I came back, I found her in my bedroom, lying in bed, with an IV in her arm.

She greeted me, "Oh hi honey, come meet the nurse."

I was a little taken back–*why were they in my room?* I came in and shook the nurse's hand, left the room and got lunch in the kitchen and went by the pool to read some magazines. At around 3:00 pm she called me.

"Hurry up, sweetie, the nurse left, and I need you right now.''

She was now upstairs and waiting for me in her bathroom with the IV still in her arm. She was writhing around, showing it to me and telling me, "Hold the IV so I can clean it out."

I took a step back and said, "Oh my God, I am totally afraid of needles. I cannot do it. I can't even look when someone takes my own blood or puts an IV in me."

"You have to, Jeremy. You have to help."

Her arm was starting to bruise. I tried to be strong, but I felt faint. I tried not to look, but I had no choice. Her panic was growing. I tried to intervene and asked, "Do you think you are injecting it maybe a little too fast?

She replied, "No, no, I know what I'm doing."

She was not listening. She injected the solution to flush her veins but did it so fast that she had three large bluish bumps in her arm. I was feeling sick.

I noticed the little vials lined up on the vanity counter.

"What are these for?" I asked.

"It's Demerol."

Ah ha, this was the delivery she was so desperate to get.

"Inject the Demerol, Jeremy. Do it fast."

I began to panic.

"I don't think I can."

"I'm in pain and the doctor told me to use it for pain. I AM IN PAIN."

I refused to help her, so she injected the drug herself. A few minutes later her eyes began closing. She was slurring and limp. I helped her to the bed as she begged me to keep her awake.

"Please, please promise. Don't let me fall asleep. Walk with me, take me around the room."

I could barely understand her. She was nodding on and off. She started to babble incoherently. She urged me to keep her awake, so we started to walk around. She was draped over me, like a rag doll, as I maneuvered her the best I could.

That dance of insanity lasted for thirty minutes. Then suddenly she was lucid.

She said looking in my eyes,

"Thank you for helping me."

"How do you do this when you are alone?" I asked.

"I just do it. I lie on the bathroom floor and I just do it . . ."

As the drugs wore off I felt relieved. She was again the woman I knew. However, she wanted more Demerol.

"I don't think that is such a good idea." I said, but she already had the vial ready to go.

In a few moments she was back in that incoherent bubble–babbling and making me drag her limp body around the room. Each time we stopped, she began falling asleep right away.

I shook her saying, "Come on, wake up, wake up please. Should I call 911?"

My concern for her grew. I started to panic. I wondered why she did not want to fall asleep, what she feared. Maybe not waking up at all? The third time she injected herself all I could think of was, what if she died right here in my arms? *What would happen if she overdosed while alone? What if the housekeeper found her like this? What if that poor dog of hers tried to wake her up by scratching her face?*

However, in a few moments she would be back in that half-lucid state, requesting more Demerol.

By midnight, I was exhausted and could barely stand. I realized that she was an expert at injecting herself and that she had been doing this a long time. Later, as I lay there in bed in the early morning hours trying to fall asleep, I re-member thinking: *Is this what my life has come to? I have traveled the world. I have worked with the biggest names in Hollywood: Elizabeth Taylor, Ali McGraw, Cindy Craw-ford, and so many more. I have dined with royalty and rubbed shoulders with the world's who's who. Now I have become a caretaker to an aging actress. I can keep her safe tonight but what about tomorrow night, and the next.*

I could just see the front page of The Los Angeles Times, "ex TV queen and cosmetic guru found dead of an overdose of Demerol on bathroom floor."

Belgium, 1964

My first memory is a photograph taken by my dad, Emile, in the spring of 1964. I was almost four years old. The photo was in front of the apartment my parents lived at the time. We were on our way to the National Theater of Belgium. My mom, Jacqueline, had entered me in a contest for the "Most Beautiful Baby in Belgium." I remember wearing my little black velvet tuxedo and black patent shoes with white socks. My twenty-year-old mother, who was pregnant at the time, was wearing a navy-blue dress with roses embroidered at the bottom that she had designed and made herself, I remember going on stage in front of the jurors. I won the contest and still have the award.

Recently, my sister told me that my grandparents did not want my mom to marry my dad. However, I guess when you are so young, and you think you are in love, nothing is going to stop you. She wanted her man, even though he had beaten her on many occasions. To secure the deal, she got pregnant. My parents were married on March 21, 1960, six months before my birth. My mom was sixteen years old and my dad eighteen.

My dad had an alcoholic father, who died at age thirty-two of cirrhosis of the liver. He used to beat my grandmother, Louisa, on a regular basis. Maybe because of his childhood, my dad and his younger brother, Fernand, continued the tradition by drinking and beating their wives. My maternal grandparents, Abraham and Marie-Louise, mostly raised me.

Three months after the baby contest, my mom gave birth to my brother, Fabrice. Then, less than two years later in 1966, she delivered my sister, Benedicte. I chose both of their names. I remember my parents discussing names for my brother and asking my opinion, and I did not like any of the names they chose. Finally, they asked what name I wanted, and I came up with Fabrice. The same thing happened with my sister Benedicte.

My mom was mostly a stay-at-home mom. To earn extra money, she accepted jobs designing and sewing clothes from various people in the neighborhood. During those times, I lived with my grandparents across the street. My grandpa was already retired from working in the mines and my grandma was the concierge in a 1950's midrise office building. They occupied a two-bedroom apartment on the ground level. I do not remember what kind of business it was, but I remember that every floor was filled with desks and each one of them had a typewriter on it. After five pm when everybody was gone, I would have a blast playing secretary. My dad worked for the city doing whatever projects they needed him to do at the time. It was an interesting way to make a living. Sometimes he would work in the slaughterhouse, sometimes a bricklayer and for a couple of years, he worked as a firefighter.

My friends laugh when I tell them that I was a perfect child. I never was grounded or slapped by anyone in the family. One funny thing I remember was spending a lot of time looking at the mirror and my mom used to tell me, "if you look in the mirror one more time, little Jesus is going to slap you from the other side." I always thought, *Wow, he is going to be very busy*. While I was spared the rod, my dad did not think twice about beating my mom. When she would pick me up at school, she would often wear big sunglasses to hide a black eye or wear concealer to cover a busted lip. When he was eighteen months old, my brother got meningitis and almost died. He did not speak his first word until he was four. The men favored him, while the women had a soft spot for me. Maybe because of the age difference, my siblings were closer to each other.

I was the loner of the family. I was shy and kept to myself.

Growing up

I do not remember a lot of joy growing up. There was constant screaming when I was with my parents and siblings. In addition, there were only occasional pets to play with. I do remember that once we got a duck. Coin-Coin lived in the house and was always biting my brother's ankles. It used to hide behind furniture and doors, and when Fabrice walked by, the duck would jump out and bite him. One day, in order to get a small taste of revenge, my brother stood up on the kitchen table and called out for the duck. The poor thing looked everywhere for him, and when Coin-Coin got close to the table and sat still, Fabrice jumped on him so hard that he ended up completely flat as a pancake, his insides splattered all over the floor.

The second pet I remember was a white and caramel colored little puppy. Once, my mother was cleaning the laundry room floor and soapsuds were everywhere, and the puppy began playing with the foam. She put him on top of the washer, but since his feet were wet, he slid and fell to the floor and hurt himself. The poor thing began yelping in pain. The next thing I remember was my father screaming.

"We're not taking that thing to the vet. I'm not paying for any of that."

My mother pleaded.

"Well, what are we going to do with him, then? The poor thing looks like is leg might be broken!"

My father took the yelping little dog, put him in a potato bag, tied it with rope and dumped him in the river. The four of us cried the whole afternoon.

We also had rabbits. My father was raising them, sometimes up to 15 of them. They were all different kinds of rabbits. Some were incredibly beautiful—all of them had cute fluffy babies. Once a week my father would choose one of them, grab it by its back legs and smash the head of the poor thing against a concrete pillar. Then he removed the skin and fur as if he was peeling a banana. An hour later, dinner was served.

Ever since I can remember, I always knew I was gay. Ironically, the subject of me being gay was never a topic of discussion in my family. I was never what they called, "in the closet." I figured they probably knew when they saw my over-styled outfits and perfect shag hair in the 70's. Nobody ever asked me the question, and I never volunteered any information. My family was the original, "don't ask, don't tell."

No one mentioned a thing when my grandmother bought me my favorite toy, Barbie. She knew that it was not for the doll itself, but to play with the clothes and hair. I remember my favorite was Malibu Barbie. She was very tan with straight blonde hair. The minute I got a Barbie, I used to cut her hair. I hid them in a shoebox under my grandma's linens. Every month I would get a new one. Back then, you could buy separate accessories like shoes, purses and wigs to play with. Then I began playing with bigger dolls so I could work with more hair. My mom, who was also very good at doing hair, owned a few wigs and I used to borrow them to play with. I also would watch her sketching out her models along with the intricate way she would design and make clothes. I know that is one skill I got from her. My sister Benedicte was almost the opposite of me—a total tomboy. Everybody was afraid of her. If you looked at her funny, she would get right in your face, insult you and spit. Fabrice was also a daredevil! These two were Bonnie and Clyde. I needed a reprieve. Thank God I was living with my grandparents for five days of the week.

When I was nine years old, the National Theater began a search to find a young actor to play the main role in the musical, Pinocchio. Out of hundreds of other kids, I auditioned and won the part. I performed in the play three days in Mons, my hometown, and then toured all over Belgium during the summer. An early bloomer, my body changed along with my voice. I was tall for my age and was growing body hair. Needless to say, I looked a lot older than nine years old. I remember seeing my face on newspapers and on television.

The play was a huge success and I saw the pride in my parents' eyes. The experience cemented my love for all things show business. The following year, due to the success of the play, the Theater made a sequel "Pinocchio in the Far West." Everybody was dressed as cowboys and Indians. We took that play all over Belgium, only playing on weekends so I did not have to miss school.

One night on the way back from finishing a performance, while seated in the back of the touring bus, one of the cast members, Jean Deham, about thirty years old and married, started caressing my leg. It felt nice, so I let him continue. Then he reached inside my pants, and it felt pretty good. Then he unzipped his fly, took out his penis, and showed me what to do with it. I remember my reaction when he ejaculated. I had never seen sperm before. I had reached the next step in my growth as a man. He never forced me to do anything I did not want to. I was never a victim of sexual abuse, and I was the one who wanted more. For the next five years, every Wednesday afternoon after school, I went to his house or office to "study theater." If you know what I mean.

I knew clearly that I had no sexual attraction to women but was attracted to the things that surrounded them. I have a picture of me when I was twelve and my cousin, Thierry, was nine. My grandma had just got a new camera and wanted to take some pictures of us.

"Wait a minute," I said. "We need a few things."

I dragged my cousin to the closet and dressed him in my grandfather's clothes. I chose my grandma's best suit with a scarf, heels, and purse and she took the picture without saying a word. I loved that woman more than I could say. For my birthday that year, she took me to Paris. We had a blast, just the two of us. We went on a shopping spree and I came back with platform boots, high knee socks and hot pants in my suitcase. Of course, I did not show that to my parents, these were not very boyish outfits.

I was also very close to my paternal grandmother, Louisa, but in a different way. I used to spend a few weeks with her in the summer and what was supposed to be a vacation often turned into a nightmare. In the 1940's she had become a widow at age twenty-eight and was left with two kids to raise. She was single for years and then she took a younger boyfriend named Jean. When it was just the two of us, we had a wonderful time together—doing her hair or dancing to music. I had my own turntable and a collection of vinyl albums and I would play DJ in the courtyard.

Jean had done time in jail for trying to kill his wife, who had neglected to take care of their two young sons, leaving them with no food, living in filth, drinking and screwing around while her husband was at work. Eventually his two kids were placed in a special home and he was not allowed to visit. He began drinking to forget about his children and as was a common theme in my life, he would become very violent. He would beat my grandmother late at night. I remember him trying to strangle her on the kitchen floor and I jumped on top of him, screaming at the top of my lungs. Another time he held her above a water well by her hair and neck and threatened to drop her.

My only real and true peaceful moments were with my maternal grandparents. My grandpa used to drink his Pastis—a famous drink in the South of France, while watching TV in the evening—then fall asleep sweetly in his chair. He died of lung cancer in his early fifties. We used to carry him to his bedroom, in his hospital bed, so he could sleep almost sitting up with the window open for some fresh air, no matter what the weather. Sometimes we would look everywhere only to find him peacefully asleep on the toilet. His mother, Arthurine, lived around the corner and every afternoon, she came to watch TV and have dinner. After the 8:00 pm movie, my grandma and I used to walk her home. My godmother was her neighbor and once I heard that she was depressed, drinking and taking pills. One day her daughter came home from school and found her hanging from the stair rail with a scarf.

Thinking about my future

I was around twelve when I began to think seriously about my future. At that time, in Belgium, kids went to school from age six to eleven. I was always top of my class in French, geography and history. I remembered choosing Cleopatra for one of my history tests for graduation and presented to the class and teacher all the pictures of Elizabeth Taylor in the movie. (Do you know another Cleopatra?) Then at twelve we were offered a year of orientation to decide what we wanted to do in life. It came to my mind for one second to be a vet, but I don't think I could have handled working with suffering animals or working with needles. I loved the theater, but my love for all things fashion and hair had continued to grow. After all these times of playing with hair, my mom and I thought it made sense for me to go to beauty school. Therefore, at age thirteen, I attended the Ecole Professional Gabrielle Passeleck, which later became the Leo Collard Institute.

For the next five years, every morning, I had high school classes, and in the afternoon, I attended beauty classes. Half of the school was for cosmetology and the other covered fashion design. For the first three years, I was the only boy in a school of three hundred girls. I was the king there. Teachers commenting often that I was "the most talented" and everybody wanted me to style their hair.

It was the mid-seventies and Unisex fashion was popular. Free love was in style. We all dressed the same and had the same hairstyles. We experimented frequently. The boys kissed the boys. The girls kissed the girls, everybody was fooling around, and the feeling was *do whatever comes naturally. We had so much fun.*

I earned my diploma in hair styling, makeup, facial, manicure and pedicure. With that degree, I could also be a beauty schoolteacher. With my grandmothers giving me money to do their hair, plus some tips I used to make from models in school, I was able to buy my own clothes. Platform shoes, elephant pants, tunics, maxi coats were all the rage. If not fashionable enough, my mom would make me the clothes. I have a photo, maybe I was eleven years old, wearing a yellow shirt with white polka dots and bouffant sleeves. My hair then was like a pageboy, so I took a razor and cut the top of my hair two inches short. I kept the back long. I thought I was Jane Fonda in the movie, *Klute.*

Since the school moved closer to where they lived, at age fourteen, I went back to live with my parents in the town of Nimy. Every day I followed the same routine. I woke up at 6:00 a.m., attempted to wake up my mom (who was usually exhausted from a beating the previous night) prepared my own breakfast and lunch and got out the door by 7:00 am. It was a forty-five-minute walk to school and I often found myself walking in the rain with schoolmates Carine and Driss, who I picked up on the way there. About twice a week, my two best friends Francoise and Michelle and I would skip the last class of the day (usually the gym hour) and go to the local bar to dance to the music of Barry White and Gloria Gaynor. (That was exercise after all.)

I would arrive back at my home by 6:30 pm. My mother would have dinner ready for all of us. I would get myself to bed by eight—early enough to avoid my father who would show up after an evening of drinking. Looking back, though he was not a fall-down-drunk kind of person, I don't think I ever saw him really sober. He could function anytime. Even with his lifestyle, we never got shorthanded on anything. Fresh food was always on the table and my poor mom used to cook different vegetables because my siblings and I never agreed on the same. We always dressed very fashionable and every summer, as kids, we went to camp (which I hated) to the Lys Rouge in Koksijde on the North Sea coast. My sister and I were good dancers, and when dad was in the mood, he used to drag us out of bed at night and play music in the living room and make us dance until he was satisfied. Of course, my mom would cringe, but we were afraid that he would beat her if she said something, so we always agreed.

His job ended by three in the afternoon. On his way home, he would go to the same bar to drink beer. It was very rare to have dinner together. On Saturday and Sunday mornings, he would leave around 10:00 am to go drinking with his friends. He would come back for lunch around 2:00, if we got lucky. Most of the time he was late, so my mom went to the bar to try to hurry him up to come back home. Upon arrival, he would find something wrong, something with the meal, something with the timing . . . anything. Without fail, he would start an argument with my mom, throwing his plate, food flying everywhere. Then the fighting would start while the three kids screamed for him to stop.

One time my mom was sitting at the kitchen table, they just had another fight, when he came up behind her and for no apparent reason he punched her on the top of her head. She lost consciousness and fell on the table. I ran to her and tried to wake her up. She regained consciousness and we looked in each other's eyes.

"Mom, why don't we leave?" I asked.

"I can't—if we leave, I'm afraid he will kill us."

That night, and for many nights afterwards I would dream of going into the kitchen, taking out a sharp knife and stabbing him. I imagined that I would just plead self-defense. I guess I was watching too many suspense movies. However, the fear of prison deterred me—I knew I would not look good in stripes!

Then one night, in the spring of 1975, a strange scream came from my parents' bedroom. The three of us rushed in to discover my mom shaking, as if she was possessed. There was foam coming out of her mouth, her eyes rolling back. My father was trying to wake her up and panic flashed in his eyes. We ran to her bedside.

"Mom! Are you okay? Mom, wake up!"

"Is mom okay, what's wrong with her, why is she like that?"

We all were so confused.

"I don't know; I don't know—we've got to call an ambulance."

I rushed to the phone to dial the number. The three of us stood like pillars of stone—in a haze of shock as the paramedics came and whisked her away. No one had ever needed an ambulance in the neighborhood and neighbors came out to watch the scene. The ambulance drove off and we suffered through a sleepless night.

We learned the next day that my mom suffered from an epileptic seizure called "Grand Mal." The doctor told us those types of seizures were rare but extremely powerful. My mom was unable to move so she stayed in the hospital for a few days. I sat by her side and held her hand. She had trouble speaking as her mouth was completely off to one side, so we sat in silence. I knew that this was a horrible way to live, never knowing when a seizure would occur or what its severity would be. Moreover, I knew that despite her condition, my father would never stop hitting her.

When mom began to feel better, our family went on our usual two-week vacation to Riccione, Italy. In our red Toyota Celica, we always stopped in Germany in a B&B for the night, usually around Munich. I still remember the very tall beds with the thickest and fluffiest comforters. Then on to Switzerland for the next stop. Finally, Riccione, our destination. It is a small town in the Province of Rimini in Northern Italy, on the Adriatic Sea. Newly built hotels and condominiums lined the Riviera and tourists flocked by the thousands. By day we would go to the beach, ride bikes or, my favorite, shopping. (I used to take one empty suitcase with me, so I could go crazy and bring back all the clothes you could not find in Belgium.) The streets were packed with restaurants, bars, hotels and discos. At night, I would go clubbing with friends from Belgium who were vacationing there at the same time. Even though my father drank from sun up to sun down, the vacation was healing, all of us together, and especially watching my mother laugh in the sun.

When I turned fifteen in September 1975, my mother decided to convert my sister's bedroom into a small hair salon. My sister angrily and begrudgingly moved in with my brother and me, so that now all three of us shared one big bedroom.

Now, with a salon, I started cutting hair for a few of the neighbors and soon word spread that I had a talent for the craft. I found myself doing hair on Saturdays and Sundays. We bought a shampoo bowl that was attached to the bathtub. I began to make some money, which I promptly used on all things fashion. That set-up lasted an entire year, until my father told me that I must give him the cash I was making so he could save it for me. Yes, right.

David

It was then that I found work on Fridays after school by 3:00 pm and Saturdays at salon David, the best salon in town. The owner, David Levy, who was around twelve years older than I was, taught me in a very short time how to be a great hairstylist and to forget everything I had learned in beauty school. This was the real world. David taught me the latest techniques including how to properly blow dry like a pro. I soon became the blow-dry king, doing more than fifteen a day. Clients left the salon looking like Farah Fawcett and Dorothy Hamill. The place was a big house with the salon in the front section. Behind that was a huge room with a kitchen, living and dining room and a bedroom, where David's mother lived. Upstairs was David's quarters with a one-bedroom apartment. His mom had a stroke and if you asked her something she would always answer,

"Mais pour moi tu reve!" meaning, "My, you must be dreaming."

However, the funniest thing was the talking parakeet who was always repeating after her

"Mais pour moi tu reve."

The staff, Driss, Brigitte and Cecile, loved each other and we had so much fun.

Soon, I could see that David was becoming romantically interested in me. We went everywhere together. We shopped in Brussels by day, and danced at the Monocle, L'Impasse, and the trendiest place in town, le Club, at night. We went to Ostende, at the North Sea to party at the "Versailles" club. Our favorite place in Paris to dance was the famous "Palace," the French version of Studio 54. The Palace was an old theater that was converted into a lavish disco. The line outside was huge. Everybody who was anybody was there. We would start with dinner at the trendy Club 7 then go downstairs for some dancing with the crowd of beautiful people, from royalty to trash. From Yves Saint Laurent to Grace Jones to Paloma Picasso, Loulou de la Falaise, Jerry Hall, Janice Dickinson, Pat Cleveland, the famous illustrator, Antonio, Andy Warhol and his entourage, Kenzo, Claude Montana, Karl Lagerfeld. I was in heaven. Gorgeous models, actors, musicians, gays, straights surrounded us. Every time we entered those doors, I felt like I was home.

One time on a trip to Paris with David, we were driving down les Champs-Elysees and his car broke down right in the middle of a packed five-lane road. Everyone began honking and screaming at us, looking at the license plate for the stupid Belgians to get out of the way. I decided to leave David by himself and go for lunch alone. I kissed him on the cheek and said, "I'm really not mechanical anyway." Then I went to a posh restaurant where I asked for a steak tartar well done. (In Belgium, a steak tartar is called an American filet—go figure.) I was thinking that steak tartar was a steak with tartar sauce. The waiter began laughing at me and then swiftly brought me a piece of raw meat with a yolk on the top. I decided I did not need lunch.

David was incredibly generous and would buy me fantastic clothes from the latest designers. He used to follow me carrying all the bags, while I would point, "I want this one and this one." Once, on a shopping spree in Paris, he bought me a Nehru ensemble from Kenzo (the trendiest rage back then) all white with red dots all over, and a hat that went with it, along with an umbrella. In addition, I could not forget the tiny round glasses to wear on the tip of my nose. That night we went to dinner at Chez Michou, a famous Drag Queen Cabaret. Michou was on stage thanking everyone for coming when he spotted my wild outfit in the crowd. He directed a big spotlight on me and said, "Even my nurse is here." After people laughed and clapped, I considered myself a complete success.

Leaving home

In May of 1978, I was preparing for graduation. I knew I needed a fabulous outfit to go on stage to pick up my diploma. Jodhpurs pants were in fashion, a mix between clown pants and riding pants. I could not find one that would sufficiently turn heads, so my mom designed a pair in fuchsia cotton. The pants were so tight down to my ankle that I needed a zipper to close them. The waist was four feet wide with an elastic. To complete the look, I wore a green shimmering shirt and silver ballerina slippers. The looks on the faces in the audience and the teachers were priceless. Even funnier was that I was first in my class in cosmetology. After the ceremony, we had a fashion show with clothing designed by the students of the couture section and hairstyling done by us. I walked on stage as a groom (with bride) in a black velvet bell bottom suit. Fashionable tattoos and earrings for men started to show up everywhere. My dad told me that if one day I got some, I would be out of the house. So naturally, the day after graduation, I came home with a bird tattoo on my arm and both ears pierced. David did the piercing by numbing my lobe with ice cubes and going through with the sharp edge of the loop. My father looked at me without saying a word. I went upstairs, packed a couple of suitcases, went downstairs, said bye to my mom and left the house. I went to stay with my grandma until summer was over. Now, done with school, I would be working full-time at David's. With that, it was time for me to find my own place. I found an apartment in a brand-new complex five minutes from the salon. I also bought a metallic light green Mini Cooper car. Life as a young adult had begun. My mom painted my apartment a different color in every room. You would have thought I was on an acid trip. Orange, yellow, purple, brown, you name it. Flurry Flokati rugs and futon on the floor completed my design. I was now responsible for rent and bills, and I felt that having to grow up fast was finally having its rewards. I had always found it oddly annoying to have such young parents. Where most people's parents were the old folks, mine were only sixteen and eighteen years older than I was. Somehow, it made me feel older. I began to track my life from the perspective that by this stage of life, my parents already had a son.

On September 1 of 1978, I turned eighteen years old. In Belgium, every male must report to the Army headquarters and I began to panic. The last thing I wanted to do was to waste two years of my life in the military. My life had just begun and the thought of me in an army uniform—I just could not see it. I decided that since I had three weeks before my appointment, I was going to try to look sick enough to be rejected. I began a severe crash diet of only three apples and three yogurts a day. On the day of the interview, I weighted one hundred pounds and at 5'9". I looked malnourished and weak. To accentuate my skinny frame, my mom made me clothes that were three sizes too large.

On my way to the train station, I could not stop crying. When I arrived in Brussels, I went directly to the headquarters and made my way to the stark grey waiting room, which smelled like rotten eggs. When I sat down, I recognized a few people from the clubs some of them dressed in drag.

Why didn't I think of that? I filled out the paperwork and they performed a short physical.

An officer called my name and said, "You're accepted."

I felt faint and wondered if I should really faint. I said, "You know, actually, I can't be accepted."

"And why is that, young man?"

Everyone in line was staring at me, wondering what in the world I was going to say.

"Well, because I'm gay."

The butch guys in line started to whistle and make fun.

"Quiet," said the officer. "I don't believe you."

I responded, "It's true. It is 100% the truth. I'm gay."

The officer wrote a note and directed me to the side. Two men escorted me to the military hospital where I was to be watched–actually, to be placed on observation. I was there for three days. The first two days the doctors performed regular checkups. I did my best to not eat or drink a thing to appear as weak as possible. Then they sent me to see a psychiatrist. He was a thin man with glasses and dark hair. I laid down on the couch in his big white office.

"So, you are saying that you are gay?"

"Yes, I am." I responded.

He nodded his head slowly, unsure.

"Well, we have a test for that."

He then placed some electrodes on my head and chest, looked at me very sternly, and said, "Okay, think about sex with another man."

While usually this was no problem at all, under these circumstances, I could not get myself to think those thoughts.

"Hmmm," he mused, "It's not working."

"I am gay, and I don't know what these things on my chest have anything to do with."

He now asked me to follow him and guided me to a broom closet in the hallway.

"Okay, I'd like you to show me what you do with other men."

"I know this is not legal, doctor. I could report you."

He began to get incredibly nervous and then took me back to his office and had me lie down again.

He paced in front of me.

"Do you, maybe, need some help to think about sex with men?"

It was at that moment that I knew. Something was going to have to happen or I would be wearing Army green.

"Yes, that would be nice," I said.

He began to undo my pants and started to masturbate me. I did respond, which seemed to make him happy. When done, he went to is desk and signed some paper, concluding that I was not fit for the army because I have flat feet. Hurrah!

Back in business and my life, David decided to take the space next door to his salon and build an annex for my growing clientele.

Once everything was in place, David took me to dinner to celebrate my new life. At the restaurant, I got tipsy on champagne, and then he dropped a bomb.

"I'm thinking we should maybe, you know, settle down."

"Settle down?"

"Yes, you know when you think about it, we're really good together. I'm turning thirty this year and I just feel that you are, well, the one for me."

My head was swirling. I began freaking out. My heart danced a thousand ways at once. He had done so much for me. He was so kind, generous, and patient and he taught me a tremendous amount about the real world of hair. I loved him but had never told him. However, I also knew that there was a huge world out there and at eighteen, I had not even begun my journey. I think I muttered something like, let me think about it. An unsettling panic set within me from that moment on.

I was an impossible boyfriend. I knew it, and he never complained. Nevertheless, some part of me knew I needed out. I decided that soon I would move to Brussels, since I was there so often. I felt I belonged to a cosmopolitan city and saw the move as an excuse to escape the situation with David. The breakup was emotional, but I was ready to go. I did my best not to hurt him but there was no way around it. My way to handle the situation with him was to be so obnoxious, that he might be fed up and end things, but I had to move to make the solid break.

To celebrate my new celibacy, I drove to Amsterdam, the city where anything goes. Clubs pounded out the best music and the fashion was fabulous. Every night felt like a Studio 54 experience.

After a weekend of partying and not too much sleep, I decided to drive back home in the middle of the night. After two hours of driving, I fell asleep and completely lost control of my car. Luckily, not too many cars were on the road besides a huge truck from Norway, who had been honking for some time trying to wake me up. It was too late, and I woke up with my car spinning out of control, a few feet from the road divider. In a flash, the car flipped and landed on the opposite side of the freeway–it was spinning so fast out it continued up a small embankment and then began rolling down.

The truck driver stopped and tried to drag me from what was left of the Mini-Cooper. I could not walk, and I was in severe shock as he pulled me out to take me to the nearest hospital. As he drove, I realized that parts of the windshield were crushed into my face, neck and arms. Hundreds of tiny pieces of glass were embedded in my flesh.

The next thing I remember was that a nurse was removing the tiny shards of glass with tweezers. The hospital called my parents and they drove there. My mom was in tears when she saw me in a wheelchair. Miraculously, nothing was broken. I think for my dad, seeing me in that condition and knowing I made it out alive, well the story with the tattoo and earing had been forgotten (not that I cared.)

November, 1978

After the accident, I decided to move to Brussels and leave my hometown behind. I found an apartment in a late 1800's three-story brownstone, behind the Hall of Justice, in one of the oldest parts of town. I occupied the second floor. You entered in a tiny foyer and on the right was a kitchen with a shower. On the left was the living area, with a marble fireplace, and beautiful French doors that looked out on the magnificent Justice Hall. The big bedroom, which also had a fireplace, had a sink. I shared the toilet, located in between floors, with my upstairs neighbor who was an older woman. A young couple, who was lucky enough to have a garden in the back, occupied the ground floor. My mom was needed to sign the lease because I was not twenty-one years old yet, the official legal age in Belgium. I decided that I needed to focus on the new life ahead of me. I was young, thin and gorgeous. It was time to dance, wear the best clothes and meet new people. (Damn, the 70's were good to me.)

My grandma, God love her, bought me a new car, a red Mazda, to replace the one I crashed. Since there was a subway, I was not sure that I would need one. I needed to find a job right away, so I asked her if I could sell the car so I would be ok financially while starting a new venture. I quickly found a job at Galleries de la Toison d'Or, just five minutes from my place. The owner of the salon, Mrs. Ring, was awarded the business in her recent divorce. She was a petite woman in her late thirties and resembled the actress Leslie Caron. She was attractive and sweet and had absolutely no clue how to run a hair salon.

She had a ten-year-old boy whom she adored and displayed the walls with his huge pictures. It was a bit uncomfortable. In the divorce, the other employees left with her husband, who was a hairdresser. I was now the only stylist there. I was happy and styled the hair for the owners of the boutiques around the galleries. Then, I received bad news from my mom that her older brother Fidel, fell at work into wood chipper. They could not stop the machine, so he came out like cat food! His wife, Janine was now left to raise her three kids alone.

Around this time, I met Nadine, a woman who was to become my best friend. I met her at La Cage—a club where my good friend George's brother, Tony, worked as the DJ. One evening, I had been waiting at the bar for George and, to my surprise, he showed up with his friend Nadine. She was twenty-five years old, Auburn hair and freckles, very flirty, big smile and just exuded warmth. Nadine was a free spirit from Switzerland.

Later that night I learned that she was living in a suburb of Brussels with her husband Gerard and her three-year-old son, Gregory. She shared with me that her husband never wanted to go out, so after she made dinner and put her son to bed, she would meet up with friends at the gay bars.

From that moment, Nadine became my partner in crime, doing the funniest meanest things possible to anybody we did not like. We were way ahead of Patsy and Edie from the TV show *ABFAB*.

What I loved about her was that with all that craziness, Nadine never neglected her son Gregory. She raised him on organic food, which was very avant-garde back then, picked him up from school every day, cooked for the family, helped him with his homework, watched a little TV and then by 11:30 pm she was at my house ready for a night at the clubs. She did not do drugs and was never a big drinker. Having always lived a healthy life and being raised in the mountains in Switzerland, she hated big cities and had to live around lots of fresh air and lots of greenery. However, she still wanted to have fun and was determined she was not going to miss anything.

The routine was for me to work from eight am to five pm, go home to grab a bite and take a disco nap from six to ten. Then I would get ready until Nadine picked me up in her little car. We would head out to the clubs until two am and then she dropped me to my flat and drove home to her family. We did this almost every night. Of course, on the weekend, we had no bedtime. We used to leave the clubs around six am and then go eat spaghetti around the corner in a joint that was open 24 hours. Nadine would then make her way home to cook breakfast and I would go to the park to cruise and have sex. On Sundays around five pm, we would go to tea dance at the "Cancan" café. Tea dancing was an afternoon affair, chitchatting, sipping drinks, and dancing from about five to about eight. Then the rest of the night we would spend at the "Why Not," the only macho dance club.

I remember so well the fantastic costume parties La Cage used to throw twice a year. Everybody wanted to attend these soirees. The first time I went with David and the theme was "Celebrities of the Seventies." David went as the French singer Serge Gainsbourg and I went as Jackie O. The next one was the "P.P. Party," pimps and prostitutes. I went with George, who dressed as a Mafioso while I took on the look of a Shanghai hooker. Another time it was a Mad Max. The best one was the "Fellini Extravaganza," where my face and hair were completely sprayed silver and I wore black shredded tulle. Well, I don't have to tell you how decadent that one was . . . Then the famous "S&M" party with George and I doing Jane Russell and Marilyn in complete get up. We always finished these soirees in straight clubs, like the Vaudeville, where everyone adored our outfits and all the boys went crazy after us. We made the papers all the time.

Within a few months, I fell in love with Willy, the owner of an exclusive boutique called Linea Bordo, located in the same center as the salon. His store carried all the big designers of the era: Thierry Mugler, Claude Montana, Georges Rech, and Nino Cerruti. Willy was 30 years old, tall, thin, with dark brown hair, and charming as hell. He was sensual, mysterious and quiet in a way that I had never experienced. I was obsessed with him and wanted to be with him 24/7. He took me to getaways in the South of France and to Paris.

Summer, 1979

In July, Willy went to Saint-Tropez for a month and invited me to go along but I could only get two weeks' vacation time, so he suggested I meet him there.

A day before I left, Marc, a friend who was vacationing there with him, called to let me know that Willy was having an affair. I really did not mind—it was the 70's after all, and I was no angel either. I left Brussels and flew to Nice where Willy picked me up at the airport with the new boy toy. We drove to Saint-Tropez and he dropped me off at Hotel de La Ponche. The difference was that on this vacation he left me in a room by myself because he was in another one for the two of them. I brushed it off as I was having a good time with friends, who were there from Brussels.

Every day I had breakfast—coffee and croissants, at Le Gorille or Senequier café—with my friends, before we would drive to the private gay beach. We used to stay there all day, lying in the sun. There always seemed to be somebody very rich who would buy us lunch and keep the champagne flowing. We would watch these gorgeous yachts pass by, wondering if it was somebody famous, or possibly Brigitte Bardot who lived not far away, might stop by, and said hello to the Queens.

At night, we would go dancing at Le Pigeonnier, a stone-lined club that looked like a cave. My vacation was over too soon and not once did I run into Willy. The day I checked out of the hotel, the receptionist at the desk looked up at me and presented me with a bill.

"Mr. Willy would like for you to pay for your room."

"Excuse me, what?"

"Yes, he said that he would like for you to pay for your room."

"But he invited me here; he made the reservations."

"I'm sorry sir, I— "

I was furious. First, he invited me to France, then he blows me off, and then he expects me to pay for the hotel.

"Look, the room is guaranteed with his credit card. If you want your money, charge him."

With that, I walked off.

A few weeks later back in Brussels I ran into Willy.

"I'm really sorry for what happened in Saint-Tropez. It was nothing but a miscommunication."

"It wasn't cool," I responded, "leaving me hanging like that."

He put his arm around me and let me into his boutique. "To apologize I would like you to walk around the floor and pick out anything you like."

"Anything?"

"Yes."

I chose a Claude Montana, $1,000 leather jacket. It sounded crazy extravagant; at that time, in 1979, my rent was $200.

Another year of good times went by working, dancing, shopping, and traveling to Paris, Spain and Italy. Every other Monday, Nadine and I would drive to see my mom, where I usually dropped off my laundry and visited with my two grandmothers. The following Monday my mom and sister would come to see me, bringing along my clean clothes.

Toronto

Then, in the summer of 1980, I fell in love with Rob Rozenscweig—a gorgeous guy in his early twenties, blonde hair, green eyes with a perfect face and a body to match. He was only in Brussels for a week, returning from a vacation in Israel, and then on his way home in Toronto.

We met at La Cage and it was love at the first sight. He was so American looking. He looked just like Jon Erik Heksum. We spent every minute of that week together. He spoke no French and I spoke no English. However, if you are in love, who needs words, and the sex was beyond fantastic.

After he left for Toronto, I did some thinking and at the end of the month, I decided to move with him to Canada. In September, I sold my belongings to one of my exes, Marc Labeuque. He also took over the lease on my apartment and later bought the whole house and the one next door. He then transformed the two places into "Les Larmes du Tigre," (the tiger's tears) the best Thai restaurant in Brussels, where Nadine became the manager.

I bought my plane ticket and went to see my mom. "Mom, I'm leaving Brussels. I'm going to try to make a new life in Canada."

She looked at me and said, "Oh! Ok that's nice, no worries here."

She knew better than to try to stop me. My mom never seemed worried about me. She always told me that I was born under a lucky star. Of course, Nadine said everything to stop me, but my mind was made up.

My mom, my sister, and Nadine came to the airport to say goodbye. We were all in tears. When I arrived in Toronto with my big suitcases, Ron was waiting for me at the airport. I was lucky that immigration had not stopped me. What I did not know was Ron was living with his uncle and aunt, forty-five minutes outside Toronto, in a town called Hamilton. His family accepted me like theirs.

Hamilton was a total cultural shock. Although it was a small town, everything was a hundred times larger. Huge supermarkets, sprawling car dealerships everywhere and there was just so much openness. I found life much easier when I had so many choices.

After a few weeks, I realized that I needed to work, and I wanted to move to Toronto. Ron said he could not leave his family no matter how much I was attracted to him. I knew that small town life was not for me. Within a week, I found an apartment on Bleecker Street in midtown Toronto and a job at the Denis Bouchard Salon.

Shortly thereafter, I began an affair with Denis, who was a handsome French/Canadian. I did not know anybody, and I found that the city was not friendly to French-speaking people. At night, I would go to clubs like Katrina's or Stages, trying to meet people.

Then in November, winter came overnight. I woke up one day with three feet of snow at my door. That did it for me. What was I doing in a city that did not like French-speaking people, with no friends and crazy bad weather? I went for a few days to Montreal to see if I would like it better. Well, the weather was even worse and there is another city underground for you to escape the coldness!

I decided on the spot I would move to either Los Angeles or Barcelona. I called Nadine for some advice.

"You think I'd like Los Angeles or Barcelona better?"

"Why don't you come home? We all miss you terribly."

"But I want to travel. I want to see Los Angeles. I want to see it all!"

"Look, you have an open ticket. Why don't you just come home for a few weeks?"

"But why should I go to Brussels first? I am much closer to California here. On the other hand, maybe I should try Vancouver. I needed to make a decision fast."

"Yes, but if you want Barcelona you can stop in Belgium first," Nadine pleaded.

She had a point, so I went home. I had no idea I would spend the next five years there.

Brussels again

I left Toronto without looking back. Nadine picked me up at the airport and I stayed with her a few days. Then it was time to start looking for a place to live before my next move. I absolutely thought that a few months later I would be on my way to a different country. During my absence, Nadine had become friends with Daniel and Richard, two of the owners of Caridan, the most prestigious hair salon in Brussels. The third owner, Jacques Careuil, was a big TV celebrity, the Ryan Seacrest of his time. The salon was in an Art Deco house located across the boulevard from the R.T.B television studios. I interviewed with Jacques and was offered a hairstylist position on the spot. I called all my old clientele and invited them to the salon. I was booked the day I started.

The first floor of the salon had three rooms, one for cuts and styles, the second space was colors and shampoos and the third was a small atrium with hairdryers and manicures-pedicures, all looking on a beautiful garden with a central fountain. The second floor was an apartment occupied by Maryse, one of the main hairstylists and her husband Serge, a police officer. The third floor was Jacques Careuil's private quarters when he was in town. We used to see him once a month when he went to the studio; the rest of his time he was living in Ibiza, Spain. Jacques was also the moneyman and we used to go up to his office to have a little chat with him and pick up our paycheck. The interior of the huge foyer and bathroom was clad in green marble. It was such a beautiful house and was classed historical. This was a very high-class salon with top clientele.

In the meantime, my mom was getting worse and experiencing more seizures. She had stopped taking her medications but continued to drive. When I would visit her, I would notice that her mouth sometime pulled to one side as if she had had a stroke. I argued with her about driving, but she was stubborn. My dad's physical abuse was still ongoing, yet even with all that, she visited me regularly—every other Monday she came, along with my sister and her new boyfriend, Concetto.

During that time, I became very good friends with Guy and Bruno, two people I used to despise before I had moved away. What is even funnier was that they used to hate me too. (Both for no reasons, whatsoever!) But, when Nadine started going out more and more with Daniel and Richard, I guessed the time was right for me to hang out with new friends. I do not remember exactly how it all came to be, but the three of us became very close. Guy, was nicknamed "Maggy Cartier" because he wore Cartier accessories from head to toe, and Bruno, who worked for a while as a hairstylist in a place called "Romainville," got the nickname "Beatrice de la Romainville" aka Bea (don't ask!) I became "The Little One" because they were four inches taller. Soon we became the Three Musketeers.

Many of the Gays hated us. We were monsters and were so vicious to other ones. We had so much fun. I had rented this beautiful apartment in a 19th century building two blocks from The Grand Place of Brussels, which is the main square, and easily one of the most beautiful in the world. My two-bedroom apartment had high ceilings and French doors, parquet floor, three marble fireplaces, and beautiful hardware throughout. Of course, back then I hated the look, it was too traditional for my taste. This was the beginning of the eighties when, style-wise, in my opinion, everything became ugly. Under my supervision, my mom and Concetto painted everything in blue-sky lacquer, including the hardware. We also installed slate blue carpet. It was also the start of the loft craze. Everyone wanted a big space with no furniture. My living room was designed with a sofa covered in a white sheet and a ten feet tall fichus tree. In addition, on the mantle, was a big martini glass with a fish in it named Nazimova. For a while, I even had a blue teacup rabbit named Alexis de Rede. He was the same color as my carpet but was possibly very unhappy because one day he committed suicide by jumping from the Juliet Balcony.

I was still seeing Nadine occasionally, but now to make extra money, she was working as a high-class prostitute. She worked Uptown, selected her own clients and was making good money. No one knew but me and when I was out of town, she used my apartment to meet customers. I found this all very exciting. One day I broached the subject with her.

"So, do you think this is something I could do?"

"Of course, you could! Head over to the Place Fontanas, someone will grab you in a minute."

And with that it was settled. You did not have to twist my arm.

That night I walked ten minutes from my apartment to the Place Fontanas, where many of the gay escorts worked. It was a small plaza lined with some older gay clubs and cabarets playing Drag shows. I was dressed in jeans and a t-shirt. Once I arrived, I found that there was far less competition downtown for the men than the women uptown. In about five minutes, I picked up my first customer, a broad man maybe in his early forties with a baby face and rosy cheeks. We went to a hotel nearby and when done, he asked if he could see me again and to make it more personal, he invited me to his home. I began to see him once a week. He was very shy and sweet and the money he paid me was so good that I never went to work at the Place Fontanas again. He lived in a fantastic condominium across the lakes in Ixelles (a chic suburb of Brussels.) I would go to his house to have drinks and supper, and then we would have sex, which I found easy because I did not have to touch him. In addition, it was over and done within ten minutes.

I was seeing him four evenings a month. I was making very good money as a hairstylist, but with that extra cash, I found I was able to travel everywhere. The great thing about Brussels is the location, in the middle of everywhere.

Two and a half hours to Amsterdam, an hour and a half to Paris, and three hours to Germany. Moreover, it was easy to take vacations in Ibiza, Marbella, Mykonos and Barcelona.

My friend Bea also became an escort in his spare time, and we used to swap our craziest stories. We also continued creating mayhem wherever we went, like going to the gay saunas and locking the door with people inside the steam room or throwing water over the people having sex in the private rooms.

One time in Antwerp, we were dancing at Marcus Antonius disco and Bea had the idea to go to this S &M Club called Boots, which was in an old factory. While there, we found a trap door with a ladder that led to the basement. The basement contained rooms with chains and slings. Seeing another opportunity to cause trouble, we swiftly removed the ladder, hid it and closed the trap. Another time Bea and I and somebody else (I don't remember his name except that we used to call him Catherine, because he wore his hair like

Catherine Deneuve, the only similarity, believe me) were in Ibiza and we decided to rent motorcycles. One night we went out to the clubs. There were two cute guys, and we pursued them heavily but got no response. Catherine who did nothing but stand there like a carp fish got both of them.

"Oh no, that bitch is not getting away with it, revenge is the "word du jour," Bea said. We were so pissed off that we left the club and went back to the port where we were parked and threw his motorcycle in the water. Then back to the hotel, which was a twenty-minute ride to the other side of the island. The next day we went for breakfast, and whom do we see walking down the street completely exhausted? Catherine. He said he could not find his motorcycle, had no money for a taxi so he had to walk all the way back from the town to the hotel. We never told him the truth. It still makes me giggle.

Another time, we made our way to Sousse in Tunisia. I told Bea "We need to work on our tan the minute we arrive."

"We have a very private beach for guests only," the concierge, told us when we arrived at the hotel. Once there, fences surrounded the place. I would bake in the sun wearing a thong (it was the 80's) laying on a huge Zebra sheet next to a Louis Vuitton beauty case. I had long blonde hair and two earrings. I would lie on my stomach, legs spread apart with the water gently brushing up against them. Bea, who was more sensual, began imitating Brigitte Bardot. He sat on his heels and covered his chest with his hands. He used his towel as a turban and began to blow kisses to dozens of guys on the other side of the fence. (Talk about "Suddenly Last Summer" movie.) Out of nowhere, a little rock hit me. I did not pay much attention to it. Then a bigger one, then a bigger one. I looked around and saw a bunch of women screaming and insulting me in Tunisian. They looked furious. The men on the other hand were going crazy, whistling and holding their crotches. Suddenly, two police officers arrived on horses to see what was going on.

"Sirs, for your own safety, you are going to have to either cover yourselves or leave."

I spoke up. "But it's a private beach. We can do whatever we want."

The crowd continued to grow, in size and in volume. The police officers were insisting,

"You cover up or it's the police station,"

We decided we had better get out of there and fast.

That night after dinner, we were walking on an empty street when, out of nowhere, ten guys showed up. We looked at each other and thought this is it; we are going to die or be sold at a slave market.

"I would love to be Scheherazade and wear veils all the time," Bruno said. At first, we feared they might want to beat us up. However, to the contrary, the leader of the pack, who was drop dead gorgeous, told us they could protect us when we went out at night. The only thing they wanted in return was to have sex. Well, well! We took the deal. We were going to be there for ten days and I was not going to spend all my time in my hotel room. We had the most fantastic time every night.

The eighties

By 1982, the mood of clubs had changed, and with the trend from London, came a new sound called New Wave. Disco was over. The music, clothing and hairstyles were completely different. Within no time, we all had big hair and wore big clothes. The style was now called 'the new romantics." The stars of that era were Boy George, Spandau Ballet, The Cure, Depeche Mode and Eurhythmics, and of course new clubs in Brussels were popping everywhere, like the Mirano, Le Pluriel and le Garage.

One day that year, while eating my breakfast at the salon, and reading a weekly magazine called Paris-Match, I came upon a 10-page article on the new gay cancer that was mostly found in New York, Los Angeles and San Francisco, but was spreading fast all over the world and only gays were catching this disease. Looking at the pictures of these poor people deteriorating and dying I started to cry. WTF? I thought. We going to die because we having sex? I put the magazine in my station and started asking clients if they knew anything about it. Half did not care and the other had no clue. How ironic that four years later, I would be doing Elizabeth Taylor's hair, the most famous advocate in support of gay rights and the fight against AIDS.

However, it did not go away. Week after week people were dropping like flies. The scariest part was that there really was no information on how to protect yourself besides that it came from unprotected sex, possibly from saliva and possibly from a blood transfusion. No gay men I knew cared too much because this this was only in America. With no information available, I started using condoms. Eighty percent of the people I slept with refused to use them, but I said no, I was not going to take a chance with my life. After oral sex, I would use some whiskey to rinse my throat thinking that the alcohol might kill the virus. That is how uninformed we were. With my sexual life turning upside down, I focused on my work at the salon, I saw my first client at 8:00 am and was out by 6:00pm. I was very close to Jacques' mother, who used to come once a week for me to style her. She was beyond wild, making fun of everybody. We laughed so hard, sometimes I could not do her hair. I was on the floor and the more I told her to stop, the more she was making fun! Daniel, the owner, was furious with us but did not dare to say anything because she was the queen mother. He was also jealous because many of his important clients came to me now, knowing that they could look fantastic in 30 minutes instead of 4 hours. It is also around that time that Jacques started to get the hots for me.

He called me in his office one day and said, "I'm in love with you, and I want you to be my boyfriend."

Thank god, I was sitting down. I mean this came out of nowhere.

"I want you to come and live with me in Ibiza and once a month, when we are back in Brussels, you can take care of your clients that week. What do you think?"

What do I think?

I did not know what to say. Here was another one who wanted to put a leash on me.

"I feel very flattered, but I have to think about it," I said.

The following week I told him that I felt I was not ready for a relationship and could not leave behind all my clients. Although the idea of semi-retirement in Ibiza was very tempting, I was too much of a wild horse and having too much fun with my friends to be trapped with someone 24 hours a day even in Ibiza. Well especially in Ibiza.

Back then, Ibiza was fantastic. There were no big hotels in the old town. We used to rent a room in a little pension, or in someone's house. We rode the bus to go to the beach, usually around 1:00 pm. The bus dropped us by the side of the road and we walked through a little forest to reach the beach. The straight beach was on one side and the gay one was on the other. We used to stay there until 7:00 pm when the last bus would pick us up. Of course, the whole thing was a big cruising paradise. You could go to the woods, right behind the beach, where people were having sex behind trees or bushes. Nobody cared. God, what libido we all had. After a little sex, or a lot, we would head back to our place to get ready, and then go for cocktails and dinner around 11:00 pm. Then, we would go dancing from1:00 am until the sun came up.

I remember once going to Ibiza for two months. In July, we would catch the Northern crowd: British, Scandinavians and Germans. Then in August, it would be the Greeks, Spanish, Italians and French. We danced at le Pasha and club KU, this fabulous disco outside of town. It was an outdoor club at the top of the hill. There was a huge pool in the middle, and a big dragon with an open mouth as a slide. Amphora, the gay club in old town was on the highest hill. They opened at midnight and were empty until 1:00 am but after that, you could not move an inch. There was a darkroom to have sex between songs. That room was always so busy. Outside the club were some ruins where people used to go cruising. One time I started to make out with some hunk and another one joined us, and another, and fifteen minutes later, I was counting eighteen guys all around us. It had become this huge orgy, and suddenly someone screamed, "The police are coming." Everyone, in all states of dress and undress began grabbing their belongings and started running around like chickens with their heads cut off. It was funny because not everybody got their own clothes, and some of them found no clothes at all. What a sight to see naked behinds rushing this way and that, scrambling to avoid the police. No wonder I am not allowed in Spain, Greece or North Africa.

Mykonos was a similar experience. There was only one great club in the village called Pierro's and it was so fun. Nobody cared if you were straight or gay. There were no hotels in town, so usually you stayed with the locals. I would walk through the village where the owners would put a sign outside of their house that read "Room for Rent." That is where I stayed. Very early in the morning, the locals used to touch up the streets with that special white paint they used, and when you woke up the whole town was clean, white, and bright. We would take the bus to the dock where we would wait for a small boat to take us to the beaches. It was just a tiny little boat (with maybe ten people) and they dropped you in the water by the beaches. The boat would drop you at Paradise Beach if you wanted to go to the straight beach or Super Paradise Beach for the gay one.

In town, there was a café carved into the rocks. You entered from the street, and the windows, carved into the rocks had no glass. We loved to get there before sunset for cocktails. They blasted Maria Callas's arias while the sun went down. It was magical.

Alain

On New Year's Eve 1983 in Brussels, I spotted this adorable cutie at la Cage. His name was Alain. He was dancing by himself and looked like new fresh meat. He was about 5'9" with sandy light brown hair. He had a great natural body. Sexy and straight looking. Everyone was after him, because we had never seen him before. Of course, when I decide I want something, I go for it. One, two, three, he is mine. Alain and I stayed together for two years. He told me he was 21 years old and was in school. A few months later, I discovered that he was 18. He was still living with his parents and was meeting me after school at my place around 6:30 pm. We would go for a quiet dinner, Italian or Chinese around the corner of Brussels's Grand-Place. Everything was new to him. I think I was his first official boyfriend and, as was normal for our age, the only thing on our mind was sex.

He could not keep his hands off me. We did it everywhere; in alleys, buses and public bathrooms.

I introduced him to Hollywood movies, the latest fashion, all the new clubs and restaurants, to a new circle of friends and, generally, a more sophisticated world than he was used to.

It took me a while to realize how much I was in love with him. (Of course, I never told him.)

I stopped seeing my "benefactor" the minute Alain and I decided to be together.

His parents didn't know he was gay. He only slept at my place on the weekend if I decided I was going to be in town. I told him that my friends were always going to be first because one day if we broke up, I needed them to be there.

(Ah, the stupid things we do or say when we are young.)

I also did not want to have my freedom taking from me. I was still having too much fun with Maggy and Bea on our trips to Paris at le Palace or Amsterdam at this fantastic club named D.O.K. Going to concerts to see Grace Jones, Diana Ross, David Bowie, Tina Turner …

One day, my mom called me to announce that my brother Fabrice was getting married to his fiancée, Veronique. So, on the wedding day, March 3rd, 1985, Nadine and I went back to my hometown for the wedding so I could act as his witness. I stopped by my parents' house to do my mom and my sister's hair, then on to city hall to sign the papers and then to church. I was extremely surprised to see my father going there since he does not believe in God or anything to do with religion. My mom always wanted to be married in church. In my hometown, we have one of the most beautiful cathedrals, named Sainte-Waudru, which is a fine example of Gothic style, built in 1450; it took 236 years to be completed. When my parents inquired to get married there, the priest asked for a small donation for the church. True to form, this triggered my father, who flew into a rage, telling my poor mom that she can forget about getting married there or any other churches. Anyway, Fabrice and Veronique 's wedding was wonderful.

Back to Alain

We had a wonderful thing going until one day in January 1985 when I woke up and decided that I needed more space. I just felt that there must be something bigger out there for me. I could not stop thinking about what Alain and I saw when we watched on TV the opening and closing ceremonies of the 1984 Los Angeles Olympics games on TV. Every little thing looked so glamorous, tempting and inviting. Right there, we decided that maybe we should go on a vacation the following summer. I thought about it all the time and I could not wait any longer. I had always been drawn to movies and glamour and somehow just knew that the life out there was for me. In an instant, I realized I was going to fulfill my life-long dream of becoming an American citizen and working with movie stars. Of course, I could not take Alain with me. He was still in school and living with his parents. Deep down, I knew he also dreamed of leaving Belgium, yet I knew I had to leave him. Therefore, I did what I knew best. I pushed him away from me. It was heartbreaking, because I really loved him. There was no reason to break up besides the fact I was moving. Nevertheless, of course, I never told him that. I became mean, ruthless and obnoxious. I treated him so badly that by summer he could not take anymore and finally broke up with me. I remember what I said to him. "Well, since you're breaking up with me, I'm moving to Los Angeles.

Photos from family album. Top: 1960, My parents wedding day; Bottom left: me in 1961; Bottom right: 1964, me and my mother on the way to the National Theater for the most beautiful baby in Belgium

From family album. Top left: school picture 1965; Top right: 1967, me with grandparents, Abraham and Marie-Louise; Bottom: 1969, in the play Pinocchio

Personal photo collection. Top: With Fabrice and Benedicte in the
mid-seventies Bottom: me with my grandmother Louisa

1979, Saint-Tropez (photo credit: Pierre Boulet)

Top: me and Bruno (aka Bea); Bottom: La Cage party, Mad Max, me with George (L) and Richard (R)

From personal photo album. La Cage Parties, Top: Punk Party with Nadine; Bottom: Fellini extravaganza.

From personal photo album; La Cage party: S&M with George.

Bottom: blond in Brussels with Alain (photo credit: J. C. La Reine)

CHAPTER TWO

Off to La La Land

It was early September 1985 when I purchased my plane ticket to Los Angeles with a departure of October 17. I began selling the few things I had in the apartment. While excited and anxious, I knew I was heading in the right direction. I needed reassurance and I needed it quick. Nadine gave me the phone number of a famous and very expensive psychic in Brussels. When I got to her apartment on boulevard Anspach, the first thing she did was to borrow my watch, to pick up the energy from it. I did not tell her anything. Within a few minutes she began to speak.

"By mid-October you will move to a city on the West Coast of the US. It will be by the water where it is sunny all the time."

I was floored. However, I tried to show no signs of emotion—nothing that would tip her off. She continued.

"You will start working for a famous hairstylist who wears a hat and has long hair. He is going to take you with him all over the country, doing television shows."

My stomach was doing flip-flops. I could not believe what she was saying. I felt it was just too good to be true. She kept going

"I see movie stars, limousines, planes, and a nonstop schedule. Then in two years, you will meet somebody younger than you. He is tall, thin, light eyes, light hair. He goes to work dressed in a suit and carries a briefcase. You will live in California for five years and then move somewhere on the East coast by the water where it is sunny all the time, maybe Miami. However, you will make a stop in between. I am not sure where, but your new partner is going to take you there. You will be famous before you turn 30. Oh, also in five years, your father is going to have a motorcycle accident and will die of a head injury. (It sounded bad, but I was little happy to hear this, thinking that my mom would not have to suffer his abuse anymore.)

Then she said, "do you have a question for me?'

Of course, I did.

"Am I going to lose my hair? Do you see me bald?"

She looked at me obviously thinking, *"Are you for real?"*

I started to say my farewell to my friends, knowing this time, I was not coming back.

Nadine was devastated, and my mom was like "well, here we go again."

My boss, Daniel, was upset and jealous, because unlike him, I had the guts to leave everything behind and move to the U.S. (That had always been his goal.) My clients were so sad and so happy at the same time. This time truly felt different. I was not leaving for somebody, I was leaving for myself.

October 17 arrived. Nadine, my mom, sister, brother and I drove from Brussels to Schiphol international airport in Amsterdam where my plane was leaving. I did not know then that after that moment, I would only see my mom alive one more time. As I boarded KLM Airlines, I began thinking about my future—realistically. I did not speak English, I had no papers and I had no job. Should I be worried? (Yes.) But I wasn't. All I had was an address of a motel to stay in Hollywood. That was the full extent of my plan.

I landed at LAX airport with my big metal army trunk, hoping customs would not stop me. I thought that anyone who took a good look at my luggage would know that I had no plan to leave. With my lucky star, nobody stopped me. It was 95 degrees outside with the Santa Ana winds blowing and there I was, wearing my Brussels winter clothes, leather jacket, boots and corduroy pants. I hailed the first taxi I saw and handed the man the address to the motel. We drove on La Cienega Boulevard to get into town. We turned a corner over a hill, and then bang, for the first time ever, I saw the city—long sprawling, as far as the eye could see. Then, there it was, the Hollywood sign, perched high atop a mountain.

This is it! I thought. There is no turning back. I was in the glamorous city. I thought of all the movies I saw about Hollywood, the stars, the fashion, the money, the glitz.

The taxi dropped me at the corner of Highland Avenue and Sunset Blvd. at the Saharan Motor Hotel. It was cheap and dusty but would do for the time being. I booked a room for three nights, struggling with barely any English at every turn. I showered, changed and made my way to Sunset Blvd. I took a good long look around. I simply stood there and began to cry. Lines of honking cars and seedy people popped out of grimy fast food joints. Homeless people shoved past me with their broken-down shopping carts. This was not the Hollywood I was expecting.

I did not know what to do. I reached into my bag and pulled out an article I had brought with me about West Hollywood, the local gay neighborhood. I had a map and started walking. I reached the corner of Santa Monica Blvd and La Cienega, and bang, right there, the gays were everywhere. Great looking men, restaurants, boutiques, hot clubs and greater looking men, suddenly I did not feel so lost. I walked around the streets and I saw a sign that read, "Studio for lease on Larrabee Street." I knocked on the door wondering how I would communicate, but luckily the manager, a French woman, told me that the rent would be five hundred a month. The place was furnished and had a window that looked right at a wall. I knew—in the pit of my stomach—that I was a long, long way from home—and a longer way from my gorgeous place in Brussels.

As I walked away, I realized I had better look for a job and soon. At these prices, my measly $3,000 in savings would drain fast. I went back to my seedy hotel, only this time with a taxi to pick up my trunk so I could move to my new place. My first night in my new apartment, I fought with the roaches that were coming out of the wood paneling behind my bed.

My second week in town, I bought a little Vespa motorcycle. I drove the streets of Beverly Hills and was dazzled. Rodeo Drive was like a movie set. I felt like I was living in the TV show "Dynasty." Perfectly dressed women that looked like Joan Collins and Linda Evans strolled by. The streets were lined with Rolls Royce, Jaguars, Mercedes and Limousines. The clothes were gorgeous and expensive. I was totally home.

Every night, I went out dancing to Rage, the Revolver, Studio One, and The Probe, trying to meet people, have protected sex and make friends.

I began watching TV nonstop, just trying to absorb as much English as I could. I owe a lot to Mary Hart of Entertainment Tonight and the popular TV show, *The Golden Girls*. Once I had a bit more English under my belt, I felt it was time to make the rounds at the Beverly Hills salons. I made my way to Allen Edwards, Vidal Sassoon and Tovar. Simple and to the point, they all told me "no."

"I'm sorry, but your English is not good enough. Sorry sweetie."

"Well, you do realize that you don't have any papers saying you can legally work here, right?"

"We're not hiring right now. But thank you for inquiring."

I was heading out of the last salon when the receptionist poked her head out. She must have seen the dejected look on my face.

"Hon—why don't you go see José Eber. All the French with no papers work there."

I thanked her and made my way down the street to the corner of little Santa Monica Boulevard and Canon drive. It was the last salon, and maybe my last hope. I walked into the place. It was chic, streamlined and packed. The manager, Fabienne, a stylish tall, thin, blond French woman and the wife of Laurent Dufourg, José's business partner, came out to meet me.

"I'm sorry, we are not looking for stylists right now, but José does need an assistant." Inwardly I begin fuming. I did not want to be anybody's assistant. I had been a successful in-demand hairstylist for seven years. I did not know at the time how famous José was. Fabienne continued.

"It pays $50.00 a day. In addition, it would just be for a few months, because we are planning to open a trendier version of the salon at the Beverly Center. We will definitely need new stylists then."

I sighed. This was my only option; it was an assistant's job—or back to Belgium.

I started the next day at 9:00 am, one month after I landed in Los Angeles. Half of the employees spoke French, the other half English. The first time I met José Eber, I was neither impressed nor intimidated. We were speaking the same language, thank God. This was just a man with a hat and a long braid, but with a huge personality. When I saw him, the words from the psychic came rushing back to me "you will meet a man with long hair and a hat." When Fabienne introduced me to him, he looked at me from head to toe, puffed on his cigarette holder and asked me, "Can you scrunch?"

"Excuse me," I said. "What does it mean? Scrunch."

"Scrunch the hair with only your fingers and make it messy."

"Well, if someone shows me, I'm a fast learner," I said

José

I was now a long way from my clients in Brussels. Nevertheless, I was always ready for a new experience. Maryellen, one of the stylists, volunteered. She showed me how to scrunch her hair. I did the job, thinking, "What the hell is this technique?"

However, José looked at it and said, "That's good enough."

The routine was as follows: José did thirty consultations a day, starting from noon until 2:00 pm. Then he would instruct all the stylists, colorists and makeup artists regarding all the work that needed to be done. Then at 2:00 pm, he would begin to work with his own clients. However, most of the time, he was running two hours late from previous engagements before he arrived at the salon. Mind you, the staff was already booked with their regular clients and they needed to squeeze in all these consultations, so now everybody was running late. It was a mad house. Everyone complained.

"He's never on time."

"He's never in a good mood."

"You wouldn't believe what he said to me yesterday, talk about rude."

Up to now, I was one of the few people who never judged him. I have never said a negative word about him. The pressure on him was huge. The whole business rested on his shoulders and I really understood what he was going through. Without those consultations he was giving, the shop would have been just another salon, but these were bringing a lot of money. As I continued working for him, I began to realize that José was what they call "at the right place at the right time." (Now that I think about it, it was the same for me too.)

José was the biggest of all of them. Hollywood stars filled the salon daily. He cut their hair and I blew it dry. The first few weeks I met Farrah Fawcett, Cher, Ali McGraw, Linda Gray, Victoria Principal, Sally Kellerman, Jaclyn Smith,

Stevie Nicks, and Linda Ronstadt. Suddenly everyone I saw on TV was part of my regular everyday life.

José was from the south of France and had started doing hair in Paris. Then just like me, he decided to move to Los Angeles in the seventies. One of his first clients was Farrah. He took her away from that famous blowout hairstyle and started to" scrunch "her hair into that fantastic mane. Then, Victoria Principal asked him to cut her hair and José said, "Ok, but I will do it on TV." After that, the rest was history.

The rumor began to spread throughout the salon that Fabienne was stealing money. Everybody told me to "watch your tips." It was odd because while José was living in a one-bedroom condominium in West Hollywood, (gorgeous mind you), Laurent and Fabienne were living in a big house in Beverly Hills. In addition, Fabienne was always dressed from head to toe in French designer clothes. However, I never witnessed anything. Back then, they were always good to me.

On my first day at the salon, José asked me if I wanted to accompany him for two house calls that evening. He did not tell me who it was.

"Here's my car keys, go get my Roll-Royce in the garage and bring it here, to the alley," he said. "And if you scratch it, I will kill you!"

What? I used to drive a Mini Cooper with a stick shift and he wants me to drive that giant of a car?

"Sorry José," I said. "I don't want to be responsible for the wellbeing of your baby and I've never driven an automatic car in my life."

With that, we both went to the garage. The first stop was at the Westwood Marquis Hotel.

We were running late and quickly made our way to the top floor.

We entered a large suite where a couple of rock and roll girls were sitting around in the living room. They greeted me and attempted to communicate with me—I cleverly used my one or two words of English. José went into the bathroom and closed the door.

As we rode back down the elevator, he told me he had just done Stevie Nicks' hair. Then we drove along Sunset Boulevard to the east gate entrance of Bel Air. Beautiful trees lined the streets. We were driving on Nimes road, and then suddenly, we stopped at a gate.

José rang the buzzer, and said, "Hello darling, it's José."

The gate opened, and we went up to the right to park. We pulled into a California country ranch house. Nothing too fancy. You could not see the house from the street. Very low key for Bel Air. We were ushered into the house where I waited in the kitchen while José went upstairs to do the client's hair.

I still did not know whom he was meeting. After a while, José called me to help him with the rollers. I went upstairs, and there in the bathroom was this dark, with silver strikes, haired woman. She was sitting in a chair, wearing a bathrobe and doing her makeup.

José introduced me, and as she turns around, says in a squeaky voice, "Hello, I'm Elizabeth, nice to meet you."

"Hello," I answered back as Elizabeth Taylor offered her hand for me to shake.

As we drove back in his Rolls, I could not believe how my life was changing.

I had just met the biggest star of them all—on my very first day on the top of that.

Very quickly, I became best friends with Danielle, a fantastic colorist from Paris. She and her son, Olivier, had just moved to California on October 15, just 2 days before me. She came to Los Angeles already knowing she had a job at the salon. Her English was not much better than mine was. I think Laurent and Fabienne contacted her in Paris and offered her the colorist position. She had a unique coloring technique for doing blonds. She invented what they called Balayage. A new way of coloring hair like you were painting with a brush. It is a widely used technique now but back then, she was the queen of it. She would have three or four clients in her chairs and each one of them was done in twenty minutes. We went everywhere together, restaurants, shopping, and beaches. We did have a lot of fun. At that time, Olivier, who was a teenager, was giving her a lot of trouble and I was happy I could give her some moral support.

In my first year, José was very hard on me. He was incredibly strict, and nothing was ever good enough. I would stand next to him while he would cut hair, then he would send me to get this or that like an errand boy. I was not a kiss ass; I just did my job. Maybe he was so hard on me, so I would give up, but I am not one to give up so easily. You never knew what you would get with José. The entire salon would walk on eggshells when he was working. At the time, I broke out in hives due to the stress. Nearly every week, Fabienne would tell me, "José wants to fire you, but hang on, we need you for the Beverly Center." Thankfully, I was making around $2,000 a month in tips, blow-drying José's clients and making house calls. At that time, Carl, who was José's assistant before my time, was the number one stylist in the salon. He was so attractive, great body, dark hair, dark eyes and white teeth. I was so in love with him, and I know I was not indifferent to him, but nothing ever happened. I think he was afraid of messing up with José's assistant. Well, his loss.

Then, clients started to book directly with me. I swallowed my pride, hoping that one day all my patience and sucking it up would pay off.

And it did a year later. When Carl left the salon and moved to Hawaii, José put me on the floor as a hairstylist in Carl's station. Then, José started giving me all the best clients. I was doing about eighteen a day. We became very close, but always in a professional way, with a respect for one another. We would use the formal use of "vous" when addressing one another, which was a clear sign of respect. There was a strong bond between us. Nothing sexual at all, but he looked out for me in a very protective way, and we seemed to have a deep understanding of one another. If he was in one of his bad moods he would come into the shop and everyone in the shop would get it but me. He let me be. Yet many people told me to leave.

"He's using you."

"You don't need him anymore."

"He's taking all of the credit for the work you are doing."

However, I did not care. I was making some money, traveling to amazing places with him and was happy, so why make a change?

Where was I going to find that kind of lifestyle? I liked him a lot and we used to have so much fun. I was very close to José. I was grateful to him for sponsoring my green card. I became his number one stylist.

Back in Belgium, in April 1986, my brother and his wife welcomed their first child, Laurie. Their second one, Randy followed in July of '88.

Then one day I received a letter from the immigration department stating I was over qualified for the position. Thank God, I was already working with many celebrities; we crafted a petition that everyone signed. The petition stated that these stars could not do without me and I was the only one who could do their hair. That worked like a charm. When the Beverly Center salon finally opened, that was the last place José wanted me to go. He told me that I needed to stay in Beverly Hills.

I worked at the station next to José and I still smile remembering his routine when doing the consultations. When a client would sit in the chair, he would light up a cigarette and say his famous phrase "Are you ready for a big change, Darling?" while cigarette smoke swirled around them. They would all beam, "Oh, I love it when you speak French." They came from all over the country to experience the glamour of Beverly Hills and spent a lot of money to be part of it. People were always trying to learn more about José and his famous hair and hat. They would ask me "What's underneath the hat, is he bald, or is the hair attached to his hat?" It never stopped. I always told them, the hat was his trademark and I personally trimmed his hair when it gets too long, so I do not think the hair is growing from the hat.

One of my favorite aspects of the job was when José would take me with him to work on television makeover segments, like Phil Donahue and Sally Jesse Raphael.

On these shows, José would choose people from the audience and we would do their hair live on TV. Thank God, I am a fast worker.

On Wednesday afternoons, it was the famous "Hour Magazine" show. It was star-packed and fast-paced. Once Bette Davis was a guest, she passed away not long after, and she did not want people to see her walking because of her previous stroke, so two assistants walked with her carrying a room divider.

Bette was José's client; the day after her funeral, he took me to her condo on Haven Hurst Avenue in West Hollywood. José was good friends with Kathryn Sermak, who was Bette's assistant and companion.

"The Colonial House" was a famous 1930's building where Clark Gable, Carole Lombard, Myrna Loy and Cary Grant used to live. I think Linda Gray lived there for a while also. Bette's apartment was on the fourth floor and had large rooms with twelve-foot high ceilings. Her place reminded me of my apartment in Brussels: wood floors, arch doorways, French windows, and a beautiful terrace.

Raquel Welch was on another show, dressed in a jeans shirt and long skirt with turquoise accessories, very Santa–Fe Ralph Lauren. When she passed me in the hallway with barely no make-up on, I remember thinking *that is Raquel*? Then she hopped onto the set and took command. She sat in her seat and held a hand mirror while she directed the lighting people to move this way and that way. This went on until she was completely satisfied with the way the light was hitting her. When the cameras rolled, and I saw her on screen, I remember thinking, "Wow, now that's Raquel Welch." I would have done the same (or maybe worse.)

José used to tell me, "I can't take you with me all the time because the other stylists are going to get jealous." However, in the end, he always took the same gang, Julie,

Maryellen, Sylvie, and me, Thierry for make-up, Gary or Danielle for color.

Then, José had the opportunity to create his own line of hair products with Faberge. The two of us went to New York to shoot the campaign. We stayed at the Plaza-Athenee, a five-star hotel lined with gorgeous marble and a concierge to fulfill your every whim. I overslept the morning of the shoot. José called me from the lobby.

"Are you ready?"

I was naked and still in bed but jumped up and was downstairs in the limo in two minutes. For the campaign, they chose the Australian model Rachel Hunter. This was one of her first big jobs as a model. Vendella was there as well. (This was right before she got very famous.) The shoot went perfectly, and José was satisfied. That night we went for a good Italian dinner at Patsy's. José was best friends with Carlotta, who at the time was the queen of the nightlife in New York. After we ate, we all went dancing at the Roxy.

Miss Alfonso

Spring 1986, a client of mine, Dee Stark, was dying to introduce me to one of her friends, Alfonso. Miss Alfonso thought he was the famous cabaret singer and dancer, Josephine Baker. We clicked right away, and to this day, we are still great friends. Dee was recently widowed and was enjoying her life. She told me that since she was a little girl her goal in life had been to marry rich and nothing and nobody was going to stop her. She used to be a yoga instructor and one day the owner of the health club she worked at came and took a class with her. (Mack Stark owned a chain of health clubs all over the country and some hotels in Hawaii and Las Vegas.) Word is she smelled the jackpot and got a hold of him. They were soon married and living in Hombly Hills, a rich enclave next to Bel Air. Mack was dying of cancer and started to spend his money on call girls. Apparently, he used to go to Vegas with a briefcase full of cash. Since Dee was "frigid" I guess the guy needed to have a good time somewhere else. But that didn't go well with her! Word was, she started to move money from his bank account into hers in no time. Also that Mack used to buy her very expensive gifts that she constantly returned, keeping the cash.

It was said that he found out that she and her mother (who was also living in that house) stole $1,000,000.00. They argued, and he pushed the mother down an escalator. From that day on, she walked with a cane.

At the end, Mack was having nursing around the clock at the house. Miss Dee, who had an aversion to any sickness, told the main nurse that she was going out for the evening and when she came back, she expected not to see her husband alive. Mack died that night and Dee bought a house for the nurse as a thank you. (I heard that story years later from a very reliable source.)

I remember going to dinner with Dee and Alfonso at the Westwood Marquis. We only drank Cristal Roederer champagne—and we drank it as if it was water. When I went to the restroom, my heart started racing. Two of my favorite hunks were there. On my left at the urinal was Richard Gere, and washing his hands was John Kennedy, Jr. with a cast on his leg. When Alfonso saw the three of us leaving the restrooms at the same time, his mouth dropped to the floor and he almost fainted. Another highlight was that my client's chauffeur, Richard, used to drive her Rolls Royce in hot pants and a tank top with a bandana on his head. (So, Olivia Newton-John.) Alfonso and I would often go to San Francisco or Palm springs to dance our butts off, and then to Russian River, a small town north of San Francisco, to relax.

One time we were at a club where Thelma Houston was performing her song, "Don't Leave Me This Way," and we met the disco diva Sylvester, who was famous for singing "You Make Me Feel." He wore long braids, a black leather jacket, black tights, boots and a quilted mini-skirt. Back then, I was having a fling with the mayor of West Hollywood, so Alfonso introduced me to him as the first lady of West Hollywood. Sylvester, clearly impressed, put his hand to his mouth and went "Ooh, Ooh," then bowed to me. He was so thrilled that he took me around telling everybody that he was the first lady of disco and I the first lady of West Hollywood. The three of us had the night of a lifetime. The poor thing died a year after that of AIDS. That was such a loss.

Elizabeth

Right away, I started styling Elizabeth Taylor's hair at her home when José was unavailable.

Her home was next to Burt Bacharach, and Carole Bayer Sager: 700 Nimes Road in Bel Air. The famous designer, Waldo Fernandez, decorated the house.

You would enter the house into a small foyer, and on your right, was a staircase. Next to it was the bedroom suite where Elizabeth's mother, Sarah, stayed when she was in

town. Across the hall was Elizabeth's assistant, Liz Thorn-
burg's suite. On the left of the foyer was the kitchen and
pantry. Straight up, was the living room, which was filled
with paintings by European masters and bronze statues,
done by Lisa Todd, Elizabeth's daughter with Mike Todd.
Huge amethyst rocks adorned the coffee table. Tiffany
lamps and creamy sofas completed the look, all-typical of
California style in the 80's. A brick patio with a pool could
be seen from all the windows. Next to the living room was
a library with shelves full of pictures of famous friends and
family, along with some awards and trophies, including the
Oscars. Next to the Oscars was the famous Andy Warhol
serigraph of her.

Flowing out of that room was the dining room, and next
to the dining room was an office, which was located behind
the garage. The whole scene was very comfortable and low
key. Elizabeth's quarters were all upstairs. If I remember
well, there were two guest bedrooms that she used as closets. Then, her bathroom, which was long and narrow with
counters the length of the wall, was filled up with makeup
and goodies. A closet in the bathroom contained a safe
where the royal jewels were kept. Her bedroom overlooked
the garden and the pool. Elizabeth had recently returned
from the Betty Ford Center. She was very thin and very tan.
George Hamilton—a gentleman, by the way—escorted her
everywhere. I vividly remember the first time I did her hair.
She was in full spiky mode with black hair and gray stripes.
José had showed me how she wanted done. Instead of doing
the ends straight, I did them going up.

She looked at me and said with a big smile, "Oh no, we
don't do Joan Collins."

To this day when people ask me who the easiest star to work with was, I always respond "Elizabeth Taylor." I guess when you live a life like hers you do not have that many insecurities left. I found many of the young actresses incredibly insecure and thus they would make everybody's life miserable. People always ask if her eyes were really violet. I remember them to be more like a lilac or lavender.

A typical day with Elizabeth would look like this: she would book me for a 10:00 am call, I would get there, and she would still be sleeping. Nobody had the nerve to go wake up the queen. I would read a magazine, watch some TV or have a second breakfast. She might sleep until 12:00, then take a bath and we would start blow-drying her hair around 2:00. Then I would put the rollers in while she did her own makeup. She used to put a black dot between each lash to make them look fuller and, on her face, she used a tiny brush with concealer to cover every individual little freckle she could find. She did not talk too much, always concentrating on her makeup, just pleasant chitchat. Then I would go downstairs have a late lunch and sit by the pool. When she was ready for me again, I would finish her hair, and usually by 7:00 pm, she was ready to go out. Thank god, I was paid by the hour and she always gave me beautiful Christmas presents from the very expensive Pratesi Boutique. One time I arrived and Michael Jackson had just sent her an unreleased song.

She was excited and said to me, "Before we start, you have got to hear this song."

The song was "I just Can't Stop Loving You." She excitedly played the song a couple of times, each time humming with "Oohs Oohs" and closing her eyes.

In summer 1987, Elizabeth promoted her first perfume, "Passion'', which smelled delicious. A publicity tour across the country was planned and was nothing short of a crazy expedition. I was scheduled to travel with her for the first three weeks. It was a fun circus of flying, tight schedules, bodyguards, hair, makeup, assistants and organizers. At department stores, thousands of people would come to see her. We would fly on private planes, borrowed from her friends Malcolm Forbes and Julio Iglesias and were escorted by police from hotels to stores to airports.

In Chicago, surprise, we were running late to the airport. The private plane communicated that it could not wait much longer. I was in the limo with Elizabeth, and her assistant, Liz, and policemen were on all sides escorting us in. We were speeding down the streets like crazy with the sirens blasting. The car was going so fast, zigzagging right and left and Liz and I almost fell on the floor. We tried to hold onto our seats, but it felt like a roller coaster ride. I looked at Elizabeth, and she was acting as if nothing was happening, casually putting on some lip-gloss. I remember thinking that she will wind up looking like Bozo the Clown. When the car finally stopped, her lips were perfect. She was a pro.

Then, on to Dallas where we stayed at the Mansion hotel on Turtle Creek. Next, Washington DC where I cut John Warner's hair, before they both went out to dinner. He was a career politician and Elizabeth's seventh husband. Miami was next, and we stayed at the Grand Bay Hotel in Coconut grove. They did not call that woman "the last star" for nothing. Each time we arrived anywhere, it was a complete production. Hotels, department stores—it did not matter. She showed up and people went nuts trying to get close to her, touch her or take her picture. Moshe, her bodyguard, did his

best to protect her while she walked through a crowd as if
no one was there. However, she always made sure her entourage had all their needs met.

One evening, at the Grand Bay Hotel, relaxing in my
room, I received a call from her assistant, Liz. She said that
Elizabeth, who was psychic at times, told her to warn me
that a man would approach me and that I should say, "No,"
no matter what he said. I had no idea what she was referring
to. I said, "Okay," and hung up. An hour later, there was a
knock on my door. I opened it to find a tall good-looking
Latino man standing outside.

"Hello, I'm here for your massage."

I was taken aback.

"Okay, but I didn't order one. Are you sure you have the
right room?"

"Yes, I'm sure. This is the room. I was booked to give
you a massage."

"Um, okay, well give me a second and let me check."

I closed the door, called Liz and asked her if Elizabeth
had booked the massage.

She said, "No."

I went back to tell the man that he had the wrong person
but when I opened the door, he was gone.

Maybe this was her vision. I could have been in trouble
here. On the other hand, maybe he was trying to get information on Miss Taylor.

The following night, Elizabeth was having a few of us
over for dinner in her suite. She was in the mood for stone
crabs, potatoes, cream of spinach, and key lime pie, everything from Joe's restaurant in Miami Beach. Boy that
woman could eat. I went with one of the drivers to pick up
the food. Back then, South Beach was incredibly run down

and scary and looked like a retirement community. People sat on porches rocking away in their chairs and enjoying the sun.

Everyone's skin looked like a Louis Vuitton bag. Somehow, I knew simply right away that if I were to leave Los Angeles, I would move to Miami.

Two days later, we were on our way to Boston. We followed the same schedule, but this time, we took a couple of extra days for vacation, as Elizabeth wanted to have some treatments done at the Canyon Ranch Spa in the Berkshires. So, the four of us, Elizabeth, Liz, Moshe, the bodyguard, and I drove up to the Berkshires for a couple of days. It was the beginning of fall and the landscape was amazing. The place itself was phenomenal. An historic mansion turned into a health spa set in an all-inclusive luxury resort. Elizabeth had treatments all day long. She was so generous and caring that she booked some for me.

When Elizabeth was involved in something she believed in, nothing could stop her especially when it came to her commitment to AIDS. The world got so lucky when she decided to go on a crusade against the disease. At the time she got involved, everybody was turning his or her back on the issue. She was close to many gay men who had suffered, including Rock Hudson. However, the world was running scared—afraid to even address the issue. But not Elizabeth. She knew someone with a name had to champion the cause, so she took it upon herself. She went out there and fought for all the infected people. One of my biggest regrets is that I never had the chance to thank her for everything she did for all of us.

On one occasion, I styled her hair and we went to downtown Los Angeles where Michael Jackson was performing.

After the show, she had a date with him. We were backstage watching all the hubbub when Michael came over to kiss her and after that, she introduced us. In person, he was very attractive, taller than I thought. Of course, this was the late 80's and he was only on his first nose job. Although a brief encounter I remember thinking that, he was very sweet.

I will never forget the other experience I had with Elizabeth. She was going on a trip and I went over to style her hair. When I walked into in her bathroom, I needed sunglasses. Her floor was covered with boxes of her jewelry: diamonds, rubies, emeralds, you name it. It looked like Ali Baba's cavern. She was at the make-up counter, happily choosing which pieces she was going to take with her.

Back at her house, I had a funny experience with Elizabeth's parrot. His name was Alvin and he was kept in a cage upstairs. Alvin used to mimic Elizabeth's voice and scream for Liz, the assistant, who was often downstairs. The parrot would call out, "Liz, Liz!" And Liz would run up and ask Elizabeth, "Did you call me?" She would say, "No". Then Liz would go back downstairs. The parrot would pipe up again with "Liz, Liz!" And Liz would come running again. The whole thing cracked us up.

Elizabeth and I worked together so often that we had a routine. After I teased her hair, we would stand in front of the mirror and she would separate the pieces. She would lift one section up at a time and say, "Okay" cuing me to spray that section resulting in that famous spiky look. Once, while she was using the toilet, my eye caught the 33 carats Krupp diamond, there on the vanity. I took a chance and tried it on. Unbelievable. It was an Asher cut, the inside of the diamond looked like tiny little steps going down from four angles ending up at one step in the middle. I remember reading an article that, when Elizabeth met Princess Margaret of England, Her Highness had previously made a comment saying that the ring was so big, it was vulgar. Elizabeth heard of it and when the Princess looked at the ring, she then asked her,

"Would you like to try it on?"

And the Princess said, "Yes."

She tried on the ring and became entranced, looking at it in admiration. To which Elizabeth said, "Not so vulgar after all."

In April 1988, we went to San Francisco and stayed at the Fairmont Hotel. Her back was killing her, so she was in a wheelchair. As the National Chairman of ART against AIDS, she had been invited to the home of socialites, John and Dodie Rosekrans. We were running an hour and forty minutes late for the party.

Security was everywhere. Dodie commented, "I haven't seen this much security since Henry Kissinger was here."

San Francisco socialites received Elizabeth as if she was the queen. One particularly chatty one, Kay Kimpton, said, "I'm surprised how short she is."

Then she took a second look and realized that Elizabeth was sitting in a wheelchair.

While I loved these experiences with Elizabeth, I knew things had to change.

One day I told José I could not do her hair anymore.

"What do you mean?" He was flabbergasted.

"Well, she takes so much of my time. I am trying to take care of clients at the shop and work with other celebrities. There are not enough hours in the day to please everyone."

"You cannot give up doing her hair," he said.

"But what if one day she decides that she doesn't like me anymore? Then I have no fall back. I will not have built up a clientele base."

José looked at me as if I was nuts and said, "Do you realize you are the only stylist in the world who refuses to do Elizabeth Taylor's hair?"

One of the last times I was saw her was at José's birthday at L'Orangerie. Le Tout Hollywood was there. More stars than at the Oscars. She was the last one to arrive, of course. She was wearing a hat and a veil. Now that I think about it, it looked like it was the same hat that she wore at Liza Minnelli and David Gest's wedding. Anyway, in no time, she left. José told me later that the only person in the world that Elizabeth was impressed with was Bette Davis. They were sitting at the same table. Bette Davis made some kind of remark to her and suddenly Elizabeth stood up claiming that she was not feeling well, and she was gone.

Later, José sent me to do Ann Margret's hair. She and her husband Roger lived in a country house in Benedict Canyon. Once you turned up the driveway, it was a ride up to the main house. I had read that it used to belong to Humphrey Bogart and Lauren Bacall. I introduced myself to discover that she was the shyest person I ever met. She made almost no eye contact and was very soft spoken. We went to her bathroom and I began styling her hair. I noticed that she had many scars on her scalp. I mused that they must have been from the Las Vegas accident. Years before she was performing on stage and she took a nasty fall, breaking nearly every bone in her face. She had to have full facial reconstruction. Poor thing. As I was blow-drying and putting in some rollers, I noticed that she did not look in the mirror at all.

Then I was teasing her hair and spraying, and suddenly she looked at her reflection and said, "Wow, that's big hair!"

The glamourous goddess was there. She suddenly sprang to life whispering, "Ooh ooh" and I could see it was show time. She was ready to go out as Ann Margret.

Miss Scott

By the summer of 1986, one of the stylists at the shop and my friend, George Miret, decided he was going to move back to Miami where he was born. He was Peggy Scott's stylist and she officially needed a new one. José approached me.

"I'd like for you to take over Peggy."

"Oh, I don't know, José. George has told me how difficult she

can be."

Nevertheless, José simply gave me the look—the look that said that I had no choice.

"Look," he said, "You are the only one in the shop that can deal with her. The other stylists are afraid of her." At that time, Peggy was a huge TV star.

I realized that I didn't have a say so about the proposal. I understood stars. Inside and out. I felt their insecurities, what it is to look your best all the time. Somehow, they in-tuitively knew that I understood them. I was not overly im-pressed with anyone. I did not get giddy or silly when a famous person called me to their mansion in Beverly Hills. I saw each job as just that—a job. I treated them profession-ally and knew how to talk to them because I knew how to

listen. I knew how to be quiet and hear what they were saying, and maybe even guide them back to the path toward
security. At times, I would get firm with them if their insecurities were getting the best of them.

I remember the very first time Peggy wanted me to go to
her house in Benedict Canyon. She was going to a big gala
that evening and was a little nervous. She had just quit a very
popular long-running TV show called *Savannah* the year before. Everyone in town had told her that she was crazy and
that she would never work again—that all she would ever
be was her TV character. Peggy was on a mission to prove
everyone wrong. She had just started her own production
company, Peggy Scott Productions, and was writing and
producing TV movies and books.

Nestled against a hill in the canyon, the exterior of her
French Regency style blue house looked small compared to
the other mansions of the area. Peggy welcomed me. As
usual, she was confident, flirty and in control of the moment.
She showed me around the house. We entered directly into
the main room. The living room was on the left, and on the
right was a quaint dining room. Next to the dining room was
a rather small kitchen and a powder room. Straight across
from the main room were French windows that looked out
at the pool. Upstairs there were two bedrooms, a master and
one used as an office.

We made our way to the powder room to do her hair.
There was no room for a chair, so she positioned herself on
the toilet and began to give direction.

"I'd like a Gibson hairstyle."

I did not know how to do it and I thought it was the ugliest
style, so I tried to move her in a different direction.

"French twist?"

"No, I'd like a Gibson."

"No, a French twist is better."

She shook her head. I could not tell if she was testing me, but I was ignoring her completely. I just smiled whenever she said anything. My English was still not that good and I truly did not understand everything she was saying. I did a French twist. A few days later, she and that twist were all over the magazines.

The day after, she called José. She had decided that I am hers now, and that I had passed the test. She had realized that I was very good, was not full of BS and was not afraid of her.

At the time, she was married to the famous gynecologist, Dr. Henry Herman. She told me she met him when she went to pick up a girlfriend at his office. He came out to introduce himself and she said it was love at first sight. She asked him out, but he refused. He said he was not ready to date, because he was recently divorced. She told him she understood but warned him not to call her after he had dated everyone in town, and so he called her right away.

Peggy is a self-taught woman. Anytime she started a business or anything else, she dove into the process with her whole heart and gave it 100%. You could ask her a question about anything related to any business and she would have an answer or a recommendation for you. In her mind, she was always right. She was a very smart woman and was very good at handling her money.

She shared with me a little bit of her youth before she came to Hollywood. It was pleasant to go to her home, though I always felt that something was wrong in her relationship with her husband. Somehow, it just looked too good to be true—too shiny and perfect all the time. Very Stepford wives. One would say "I love you," and the other would say, "I love you more." The lines felt rehearsed. Honestly, I could not tell you, which one was vainer. In addition, she was in complete control, telling him what to eat, what to wear and what parties to attend. I thought if something happened to her, he would never make it.

My fist photo shoot with Peggy was for the cover of her book, "Peggy's Diet." She had done a photo shoot using José a few months before for that but did not like any of them for the cover. She requested that I do her hair and I made it very big, wavy and she looked fantastic. I also styled her for the last book, "Living with Peggy."

Soon she had me working with her on all her projects including photo shoots for TV Guide, Orange Coast, Good Housekeeping, and Woman's World. Years later, I also worked on a shoot for Harper Bazaar, when she was playing in a new TV series. I styled her hair for the pictures for all her photo sessions, especially the ones with Harry Langdon and Jeff Katz. She was demanding, in a very good way, because she was a pro and she knew what she wanted. Some found her difficult, but we had an easy connection because I did not care about her celebrity and I would stand up to her if I needed to. She needed people around her that could do that. I remember the first Christmas gift she gave me; a mug with her name on it and inside she had placed some cookies that she said she baked, all very sweet. Later, she got very generous with her gifts.

I went with her to every talk show where she was a guest. On one occasion, at the salon, I discovered that she was not fond of Linda Gray. She saw her, and she leaned in to me, "You know, Linda is twenty years older than me." I knew that Linda was maybe ten years older and that she looked fabulous.

Stars

I was working on Stevie Nicks when she asked me to do her hair for the cover of the Fleetwood Mac album Greatest Hits. Stevie was fun and ironically, she told me she always wanted to be a hair stylist. I remember meeting at a huge mansion in the canyon that looked like one of those blue Swedish castles. I got there in the morning, maybe 8:00 am, and it was a big to do. Every member of the group was there—getting ready in different parts of the house. I began styling her hair as other artists went to work on make-up and clothing. Hours went by and it was now 6:00 pm. Nobody was ready. I told her I had to leave, and that José would send someone over to replace me. The next day I went back to finish her hair. The album cover took 24 hours to shoot and at the end, she put a hat on her head. (So Stevie!)

I first met Ali McGraw at the salon. First class act. Ali was a wonderful person, very gracious, and very charming in person. She loved animals, which was a major plus for me. I found her to be a very refined woman—in the way she spoke, stood, posed her hands, and crossed her legs. I think she took ballet as a youngster, and I know she worked at Harper's Bazaar magazine with Diana Vreeland as one of her assistants. She was the kind of woman who could make something out of nothing. Give her a potato sack, a belt, scarf and jewelry, and she would whip it into a fashion statement.

She used to pick me up in her SL Mercedes and we would go on location for her magazine shoots, just the two of us with no entourage. Because stylists would sometimes bring her the wrong wardrobe, she would bring her own jewelry and clothes to the set. The year she was a presenter at the Oscars, she had just cut her hair short. Oh, my God everyone wanted that hairstyle.

Another interesting woman I worked with was Cynthia Allison, the newscaster on Eye Witness News and Holly-wood Close Up. I would go to her house in Benedict Canyon and play with her dog Samantha. I was the chosen hairstylist for the newscasters, including Steve Kmetko from E channel. When I was with Cynthia, it felt like I was her brother. In fact, Cynthia wanted to marry me, so I could get a green card faster.

Another fantastic woman I worked with was Sylvie Vartan. She was the tough and glamourous French singer. I had grown up listening to her music—she was *the* French singer from the 60's to the 80's and one of the first crossover singers of her time, making it big both in Europe and America. Her husband Johnny Halliday was the French Elvis Presley.

Another notable moment was when I worked with Fawn Hall from the Oliver North scandal. She had just moved to L.A. and needed a makeover because she was getting her own talk show. She was actually very sweet and had fantastic hair.

I saw her once 20 years later. She was working the cash register at the famous bookstore "Book Soup" on Sunset Blvd. I walked over and said, "Hi, you might not remember me, but I used to do your hair 20 years ago."

And she said, "Jeremy?"

It was one of those small world moments I will never forget.

Linda Gray was another first-class act. Like Ali, she was bigger than life, and so much fun. I remember styling her hair for the Life magazine story on the cliffhangers of Dallas and Dynasty. It was Linda Gray and Linda Evans both in evening gowns hanging onto a fake mountain built in the studio. I also styled her for every gala she attended. I have a picture of doing Linda's mother hair, who was a clone of Linda for Linda's daughter's wedding at the Bel Air Hotel. Linda's face was so full of expression, she was funny and always seemed to be in a good mood—always with a joke. After I left Los Angeles, I did not see Linda for another twenty years. I was in Beverly Hills getting something to eat, and I walked through a side alley as a shortcut and I could see someone from the back, on the phone. I knew it was her. She did not see me, so I waited until she was finished with her conversation.

I made my way up to her and said, "Linda."

She turned around.

"Oh my God, is it you, Jeremy? It's been so long."

"Twenty-two years exactly." I said.

We looked each other up and down. She leaned in.

"You haven't changed!"

"Neither have you." Another small world moment.

At the salon, I blew dry Farrah Fawcett. So much hair. At that moment, she wanted it straight. She seemed always a little disconnected and whiny—I did not get the best feeling while working with her. I worked on her for over forty-five minutes and the woman left me a two-dollar tip.

We all loved it when Sally Kellerman would come into the shop. She was tall and commanding—she would enter and go right to José and ask with that great voice of hers, "José, are you in a good mood to cut my hair?"

I also worked with Peter Frampton and his wife Barbara—a fantastic couple—and New York socialite, Cornelia Guest, when she was in town, as well as the multi-talented and so funny Brenda Vaccaro. Brenda did not give a shit about anybody. She had been on Broadway, TV and in movies and seen it all.

Some other highlights from those years include blow-drying Jaclyn Smith's hair. She was such a natural beauty and only came into the shop on occasion. Later, I used to braid Cher's hair. I did tiny little braids everywhere while she was getting a pedicure. Then, she slept on it and took the braids out the day after so now it looked like her hair was crimped all over. Cher was a "what you see is what you get" kind of person. She would come to the salon with no makeup at all. She was quiet and kept her focus.

I was also working weekly on Rod Stewart's ex-wife, Alana Stewart. She was a tall blond with wavy, shoulder length hair and a nice body. She was a total germ freak and was impossible with her hair. 'It's too hot. You are pulling too much. It's too close to my face!' She had an opinion for every movement I made. She needed a lot, and I mean a lot, of attention. I used to go to the fantastic house Rod had given her that was just off Sunset Blvd. She had three kids, Sean and Kimberly from Rod and Ashley, the son she had while married to George Hamilton. She had the biggest closet I had seen thus far. It was as big as a dry cleaner, and even had a machine that you could push that would bring her specific outfits. Through Alana, I met Bianca Jagger, whom I saw a couple of times at the house.

Very often, I would work with Victoria McMahon, the wife of Ed McMahon. She had been a first-class flight attendant and had met Ed on a plane ride. Victoria was lots of fun. She used to come to the salon a couple of times a week or call me to go to her house in Beverly Hills. They lived on Darryl Zanuck's former lavish estate in Beverly Hills. She would give me tickets to go to the Star Search show every week. She and Ed were big drinkers. At José's birthday party at L'Orangerie, they got plastered.

Gene Simmons would arrive at the salon in a suit and tie. He was an absolute gentleman and not the persona that you saw when he performed with KISS. He had extremely difficult hair, frizzy and out of control. He was a big expressive man that no one dared mess with. At that time, he was dating Shannon Tweed, the famous Playboy Playmate.

Joan

The first time I worked on Joan van Ark's hair was at the height of the "Knott's Landing" craze. She was a surprisingly very funny woman. Hardly anyone knew what a great comedian she would have made. She felt that to be taken seriously, you had to be a dramatic actress. The shooting was the cover of Star Magazine and it was July 8, 1986. I got to the Studio and I started working on her. I realized that she was very insecure. She never seemed to think she was good enough and had a very hard time relaxing. For all the glamour, she was just a down to earth regular girl—who happened to be obsessed with her eyelashes. I would fly with her to New York, for six hours, and she would eat peanuts and cut and apply lashes.

Once we were driving down from the top of Mulholland Drive to Laurel Canyon in Studio City where she lived. The road was like a winding snake, with one curving into another. She had one hand on the wheel of her Mercedes, and with the other hand, she was doing her lashes looking in the rear-view mirror. I was scared to death, but we made it. She was also silly and fun. She used to walk around the streets of Beverly Hills with dots of toothpaste on her face to draw out impurities. I worked with her for covers of TV Guide, Woman's World, Woman's Day, the Emmy's and every gala and party she attended. One time we went to New York where she was doing work for some charity. We stayed at the Sheraton in Times Square. We arrived, and Joan had booked a suite for her and a room for me. However, the hotel was oversold so they upgraded me. I was very happy with that. We went first to my room and it was clearly the best suite in the hotel. Huge, adorned with green marble and Empire furniture. Joan took one look and said, "WTF! Let's go see my room!"

Turns out she had been given a small suite, all in beige. I said to Joan, "Take my suite and I'll take yours."

Nevertheless, she declined saying, "No, thanks, I just checked the lighting in the bathroom, and it's better than yours for doing my lashes."

That evening, when we went to the gala, people thought I was Bob Mackie, the famous costume designer who designed outfits for Cher and many others stars. Mackie was at least twenty years older than I was. Joan was hysterical and went with it, introducing me as him. When people would look at me twice she would offer, "Doesn't he look much younger in person?"

Joan used to send me bottles of Perrier-Jouet champagne at the salon all the time. A few years later, when I moved to Dallas, she bought me a beautiful Botega Veneta leather bag. I also worked on some TV movies, including one filmed in downtown Los Angeles, with Bea Arthur, whom I loved from the Golden Girls. Everything around Bea was big. She was a very tall woman with very big clothes and a bigger entourage. I even remember seeing her walk down-town with her big feet—wearing no shoes. (My pet peeve!) The bottoms of her feet were black!

At times people thought I was Joan's son. Maybe because we both had long blonde hair. (Although I do have better lashes.) I have a picture of her that she signed saying "I al-ways enjoy traveling with you. Gives us a chance to chat about dad. Love, Mom."

Bob

In June of 1987, Missy, the receptionist at José's who had just moved from Dallas, told me that she had a roommate named Bob that she wanted me to meet. She said he was cute and was twenty-two years old. I told her I was not in-terested. I had just broken things off with this Latino named Hugo, whom I had been seeing since January.

She kept insisting so finally I gave in saying, "Fine, bring him to the shop sometime."

Well, the next day he showed up. I was in the lobby wait-ing for my client to be shampooed, just flipping through a magazine when in walked this tall, thin, blond man with bright green eyes, wearing a yellow nylon turtleneck. He looked all of 12 years old. Not my style at all, I went for the spicier type. He was standing at the desk while I sat on the bench, reading.

Missy, from behind the desk said, "Hey, Jeremy, this is my friend, Bob."

Not moving from my seat, I looked at him, nodded a small hello and kept flipping my pages. Then the two of them chatted for a moment and he left.

I asked her, "What did he say?'

"He thought you were an asshole," she answered.

I remember thinking, *good, I am not his type either, no point in wasting time.*

However, Missy would not let up. She kept insisting that we go for dinner. Honestly, I had never been on a date before. That did not exist in my world. I would have sex first and then maybe dinner, if the sex was good. However, Missy would not let up, so I finally called Bob. He had a light southern accent. I asked him out and he said yes, but ended with, "Sounds good, but Missy must come with us."

A chaperone? You must be kidding.

Two days later the three of us went out for dinner in a restaurant on Sunset Blvd. I ignored him completely, only talking to Missy. When we left, I turned to Bob.

"Be at my place tomorrow at 4 pm. Come alone."

I do not know why I said it. Maybe I did not have anything else to do. I felt that if he showed up it meant that he was interested and if not, life would go on as usual.

The next day on the dot, he was at my door wearing a suit and tie and carrying a briefcase. He was a rep for an office furniture company and did not have time to go home to change. The moment I saw him I had a flashback about what that psychic had said two years prior. He was exactly the picture she had painted, and I wondered if he could be the one. The next week I asked my friend Alfonso for dinner, so I could introduce him to Bob.

We chitchatted for a while and when Bob went to the bathroom, Alfonso looked at me and said, "He's only twelve years old!"

We had a good time together and a few weeks later Bob asked me to come to the showroom at the Pacific Design Center where he worked. His mother was going to be there, and he wanted to introduce me. I brought my friend, Thierry, the makeup artist at the salon, who had short hair (mine was long.)

After the short introduction, I could hear the mother telling Bob "Well I hope it's not the fellow with the long hair!"

At the same time I met Bob, Thierry also met his new boyfriend, Robert Jowers. Robert was sixteen years older and a Vietnam veteran. He was working with Tony Charmoli, a fantastic choreographer in the Hollywood heydays, who had worked with almost every movie star, including Cyd Charisse, Mitzi Gaynor, Julie Andrews and Debbie Reynolds. The four of us were very close friends for a long time, but when Thierry separated from Robert in 2000, my friendship with him went down the drain. Up to this day, Bob and I are still family to Robert.

Bob told me his Elizabeth Taylor story. Missy told Bob that she wanted to go out. She knew that Elizabeth was coming to the salon that evening, to have her color done. By 6:00 pm, the salon was cleared out. Bob was waiting in the reception area when suddenly he heard a screechy voice coming from the back room.

"Salad, salad, I want some salad, everybody needs salad."

Suddenly, around the corner, there she was, with a big T-shirt tied with a knot on the side with Groucho Marx face printed on, black tights and sandals. She turned to Bob, whose mouth was wide open and asked, "Do you want some salad?"

Then she turned around to George Hamilton and said, "George, get salad for everybody at La Scala."

I remember the first time I introduced Bob to Peggy Scott. I was on a photo shoot with her and she wanted to meet him. She was sitting on the floor naked with only a big scarf to cover herself. Bob arrived, and I said, "Bob, this is Peggy."

She looked at him, opened the scarf and said to him, "Say hello to the birdie."

Bob's face turned red like a tomato.

I do not remember exactly how or when, but Bob and I became inseparable. We laughed incessantly. I introduced Bob to a new world and he loved it.

One night, we went to the Roosevelt Hotel in Hollywood, where they had a cabaret, to see Eartha Kitt singing. We were seated at the first table and during a song she came over, sat on Bob's lap, and stuck a mike in his face, then asked with her famous purring voice, "And what's your name handsome?"

Bob said in his deepest voice, "Uh, uh Bawwwwb!" She responded, "Well, hello Bawwwwb!!"

I thought he was going to crawl under the table!

Bob and I were total opposites and somehow this created a balance that both of us needed.

In 1988, José wrote a book called, "José Eber Beyond Hair." What a production. The book was all about makeovers. José had to choose all of the models and they all had to be regular people; homemakers, teachers, businesspersons.

There were so many of them—all of which needed a good transformation. This entire experience took months. Everyone at the Salon was working on this book. We had to select which people to work with, and then transform them with haircuts, perms, highlights, makeup, manicures and new clothing.

Michael Childers took all the pictures for the book.

When the book came out, I was proud that the makeovers on the cover were of my work. José wrote me a personal thank you in the author's note.

Gladys

Three months into my relationship, Bob called me at work.

"You have to stop by the Beverly Center at the pet store. There's a black pug in the window you have to see."

I protested.

"Nah, I live alone and travel too much. I do not think it is a good idea. Besides who is going to take care of it when I'm gone?"

"I will." He chimed in.

Still I knew that having a dog was a lot of responsibility. I did not want to go look at the dog because I knew I would not be able to resist. A week went by and I found myself in front of that little monster in her cage. It was love at first sight. She had that look that seemed to say, "I'm up to no good, please take me." Needless to say, she was now mine: Gladys, my first dog.

Months later Bob wanted to move closer to me, but I felt I was not ready to live with someone.

I moved to a two bedroom up the street on Holloway Drive and Sunset Blvd, and Bob rented the studio next door. He slept over about three times a week. I never slept at his.

Another year went by of working and traveling, José took me to Saint Louis, Chicago, Washington DC, Orlando, New York, and Baltimore. In July 1987, my sister Benedicte got married to Concetto. My dad was livid, how dare she marry an Italian and not a Belgian fellow. Of course, with no green card in my possession, I could not leave the country, for fear of not being able to enter again.

Mom

In June of 1988, I sent my mom a ticket to come and visit me in California.

She had had a brain tumor removed a few months prior and her head was still shaved. She had a huge scar across the left side of her head. The doctors told her that a tumor had caused her epilepsy, which by the way was only getting worse. One of the risks of the surgery was that there was a 50% chance she may come out of it paralyzed. In the back of my mind, I always carried that vision of my dad punching her on the top of her head. I had always thought maybe that is what caused the tumor. I hoped I was wrong, but I would truly never know. After the surgery, the epilepsy kept returning, and the doctors realized it had nothing to do with the tumor. Sadly, she began having strokes on occasion. I wanted to do something to help. I knew that she was now wearing a wig so before she arrived I went and bought her two new ones.

I drove to LAX to pick her up. She looked so different. So pale, beat up and so very tired. Both the disease and the trip had hit her hard. She also had a bad wig on and I was glad I had the new ones to give her. It had been three years since I had seen her, and she stayed with me for two weeks.

I introduced her to Bob and, of course, she did not ask any questions. She cooked her famous spaghetti Bolognese and I invited Alfonso for dinner. I took a week off to be with her, to spoil her a bit. First, we went shopping and bought new dresses, purses and some jewelry. Then I took her to Disneyland, the San Diego Zoo and Universal Studios. Smack in the middle of the vacation, José called and said he needed me to go with him to Las Vegas to style the hair of a model for his new haircare TV commercial. He bought plane tickets for me and my mom.

José picked us up in a limo and we were on our way to the airport to fly to Las Vegas. She had never seen a car like that in her life and she was in heaven. José made small talk with her, trying to make her feel comfortable. We stayed at the Riviera hotel for three days. The Riviera belonged to Meshulam Riklis, Pia Zadora's husband—both José's clients. Meshulam was also the owner of Faberge, a huge cosmetics company, famous for the 1970's perfume "BRUT" for men and "BABE "with Margaux Hemingway as a spoke model. My mom relaxed by the pool, while I worked. At night, we went out on the town. We went to see shows like "La Cage," with all the drag queens, and "Beach Blanket Babylon." She did not understand the plays at all, but she had a blast. She especially liked going backstage to meet the cast and take pictures with the actors. She was wearing the new outfit and the fabulous spiky auburn wig I had purchased for her and everyone was complimenting her. "Oh, I just love your hair!"

The commercial took a full day of shooting to complete. Ironically, they never used that video. The story showed a plane flying, then a girl jumping out of it in a parachute. When she hit the ground, she removes her helmet, shakes her hair, looks at the plane and said, "Thank you José Eber." José was supposed to be flying the plane.

I begged my mom to stay with me in Los Angeles. I told her that we could find top-notch doctors and that her quality of life would be so much better.

Her answer, "I can't leave your father. What would become of him without me?"

I just stood there and stared at her. The man had used her as a punching bag for decades. Internally I was screaming, *are you shitting me after everything he has done to you?* However, that was my mom. Her heart was huge.

We spent the rest of the week shopping and showing her the homes of the movie stars. One day toward the end of her trip, she looked extremely tired. She said she could not sleep at all. I asked her why.

"Well, since I arrived Daisy (Gladys was our pug's name, I don't know why she called her Daisy) has been sleeping with me between my feet."

"So, move her."

"We'll each time I move, Daisy bites my feet."

"So, kick her out of the bed!"

"Oh no, I want her to be comfortable."

The day came when it was time for her to leave to go back to Belgium. I drove her to LAX to catch her flight. We said a long tearful goodbye, not knowing if this might be the last time we would see each other (at least in this lifetime.)

Dorothy

Three months later, Bob told me to stop by the Beverly Center.

"There is a Boston terrier in the pet store window that you just have to see!"

"Oh no, two dogs, are you mad? Gladys is a full-time job."

I took that dog everywhere hiding in my leather jacket, shopping, restaurants. She was the light in my eyes. In the morning, when I got ready, she wanted to know everything that I was doing as I was doing it. I would I put her on the bathroom counter and let her study my every move. I swear we had a telepathic connection. We would have long staring contests. I would look at her and say, "I love you," and she would blink her eyes until a few tears would drop. She was also just like me—full of allergies. I would give her medicine daily and say loudly, "who needs a pill?" And she would throw herself against the wall and scratch her back. She would wake up only to eat breakfast while thinking, *what is for lunch?* I worried that she was lonely during the day. I would leave at 8:30 in the morning and then come back at 6:30 in the evening. In addition, when I came home, I spend the first ten minutes cleaning the mess she left in the kitchen. I hired a trainer who came to the house to show me what to do with her.

She said, "If she uses the bathroom inside the house, don't spank her or scream, dogs don't know what they did, they have to be caught doing it. Then, very gently but strongly, you point your finger and say, "NO!" the whole consultation took ten minutes and I paid my $250 thinking, what a waste of money.

The day after, I caught her pooping in the kitchen. With my pointed finger, I looked at her and said "NO." To my surprise, she never did it again inside. She always waited for me to come home. Money well spent.

"Maybe another dog will keep her company?" Bob offered.

So clever. So along came Dorothy, a three-month old, white with black spots, Boston terrier.

Dorothy was always on her own cloud. "Who am I, where am I, let me smell the flowers!" Her face was like a blowfish with a sweet pink nose. She was closer to Bob, and even taking after him. She loved the outdoors and loved everyone—the total opposite of Gladys and me.

Moving in together

By Christmas 1988, Bob thought it might be better if we got a house with a yard for the girls. I had never lived with anybody, but I realized that we could not continue as we were. Knowing in my heart it would never work, we decided to move in together. We found a house on Crescent Heights and Melrose Avenue, across from the Fred Segal store. Moving in together only amplified that Bob and I were total opposites. Bob is disorganized and messy and could not care less about material items. He is a Sagittarius. Me, I am a Virgo with seven planets in Virgo, and my moon in Capricorn. I am so grounded and doomed. Everything must be completely organized, and I am very possessive of my things. Do not touch them.

A few weeks after we moved in together, it felt as if I was going to have a nervous breakdown. I felt it was too much for me to live with someone. I already took care of 18 clients a day at the shop, five days a week, unless I was on a photo shoot with a celebrity or traveling with José. Therefore, we were on shaky ground to begin with. Then one day, a month later, out of nowhere two of Bob's friends, from his party years in Dallas, showed up at the house, unannounced. Bob must have given them the address without telling me.

Three days later, Bob told me that he had been in love with one of them for years and that he wanted to leave me for him. He had realized after seeing him that this person was the love of his life.

Are you shitting me? Bang, talk about a slap in the face. This was the last straw. I just exploded and had a breakdown. I cried nonstop, not because of Bob and his new paramour, but because this was just an accumulation of everything going on in my life.

I could not even work or function at all. Beatrice, the salon manager, took me to her doctor right away. He prescribed some rest and medication. I remember coming home from the doctor's office thinking; damn I am stuck in this house with a year lease. I did not know what to do. I could not focus. (And trust me, that is not like me.)

To make the situation even more fun, Bob asked if he could live in the second bedroom with his boyfriend. Right under my nose. I was at work constantly and I was just too out of it to ask him to move out.

In March of that year, Joan van Ark called me. "Jeremy, I have to go to New York for a couple of days, pack your suitcase and let's go, let's have fun."

I felt that it would be a good break for me and maybe help clear my mind. Off to New York. We stayed at The Mark hotel on 77th and Madison Avenue. As usual, I had lots of fun with Joan. I told her what was happening and she made everything possible, so I could, maybe, try to forget about it.

On my way back, sitting in the plane, I did a lot of thinking. I had always believed in myself, but I never believed in God. However, I was desperate-so I made a pact with him. *If you really exist, give me the strength to wake up tomorrow and have everything that just happened be behind me and start a new day.*

Bingo! The next day when I woke up, I felt 90% better. Thanks up there. I felt stronger and my tears had stopped. I guess someone was listening. I was back to my old self a few short days later. I felt that all the crap was behind me and that I could care less what happened with Bob and his new boyfriend.

I decided to go on a vacation. I called my friends in St. Louis, Steve and Jim, I had met them the first time I went there with José to do makeovers on the "Sally Jessy Rafael show," and we had stayed in contact since. They had come to Los Angeles two years prior for vacations and stayed with me. So, the three of us decided to go to Florida for ten days. The trip was a lot of much needed fun. We met in Tampa and drove our way to Fort Lauderdale for spring break.

When I came back, Bob came to me, "I'm so sorry. I made a mistake when I let you go, and I realized that you really are the one for me. I don't know what I was thinking so please, please, give me another chance."

I thought about it for a while. Though I was skeptical, I decided to give him another chance. Everybody deserves one. He wanted to start fresh in Dallas (his hometown) and he thought I could open a hair salon there.

I was exhausted with my Los Angeles life and thought maybe Dallas might be the change I needed. I met with José the next week and told him that I wanted to move out of Los Angeles and soon.

"Are you really sure," José probed. "What about New York?"

He said that his friend, Bruno Pittini, wanted to sell his salon on Madison Avenue and that would be a "great opportunity."

We went there to check it out. It was a very chic salon and I thought about it seriously. However, after a few days of New York stress and my nervous breakdown, I decided I needed something quieter. Therefore, Dallas it was.

José, Laurent (José's business partner) and I became partners for the new venture. I went out to Dallas to look for a suitable location. Before I left, my sister called and told me that Marie-Louise, my beloved grandmother, had died of a diabetic coma. She also said that my mother was getting worse and did not know that her mother had died. I was in shock and cried all night. My grandma had practically raised me, and I wished I had been there more for both.

By summer, my friend Guy, from Brussels, came to visit us. I was hoping that Bruno would make the trip also, but it didn't happen. I was so happy anyway. It had been four years since we saw each other, and we had so much to catch up on. I took a week off and we did the town. I gave him a tour of the movies stars' homes, went to Universal Studios, and shopping on Rodeo Drive. Of course, we did all the clubs.

Top photo: Elizabeth Taylor at home (photo credit: Michel Montfort)
Bottom left: Ali McGraw (photo credit: Douglas Kirkland); Bottom
right: Linda Gray (photo credit: Greg Gorman)

Top: Joan Van Ark (photo credit: Harry Langdon); Bottom: Ann Margaret (photo credit: unknown)

Top: Peter Frampton (photo credit: unknown); Bottom: (L to R) Danielle, Sylvie Vartan, Thierry, and me (photo credit: unknown)

Top: Stevie Nicks (photo credit: Herbert Worthington III); Bottom:
with Fawn Hall (Photo credit: unknown)

Top photo: Bob and me, summer 1989; Bottom photo: 1987, my birth-day at L'Orangerie with from left, Alfonso, me, Bob, Robert (photos from personal archives)

Top left: at Jose Eber for editorial shot, 1987 (photo credit: Dominique Desrue)

Top: with Jose (photo credit: Michael Childers); Bottom: on stage for
makeovers

Top photo: visiting Marilyn Monroe's grave with my friend Guy, from Brussels, summer 1989; Bottom photo: my going away party at José's with Olivier, Julie, Sylvie, me, Danielle, Maryellen (personal archives)

Mom in front of the salon in Beverly Hills, 1988

CHAPTER SIX

Dallas

By late December of 1989, I was saying goodbye to all my clients. To celebrate my departure, José and Laurent gave a party at the Salon. I felt appreciated by these men who had seen me grow tremendously since I walked in their door just four years earlier. At the end of the month, Bob and I left for Dallas. All of us took the plane together, Gladys, Dorothy, Bob and I. Each girl had their own carrier. The flight was three hours long. One of my clients, who worked with the airlines, put us in first class. That was it, goodbye Los Angeles, welcome Dallas. I looked out the window as we were about to land. It was all white, a heavy snowstorm had blown in. All the planes were flying in circles around DFW airport, unable to land. After a full hour of circling, the girls began getting very restless. I took them out of their carriers and put them in my lap. Well, the flight attendant pitched a fit.

"It's against the law, you must put them back in their carriers. Right now!"

She stood there staring at me. However, I was not having it.

"Well, first, if they were service dogs it would be OK to take them out. Second, we have been on this plane forever. We left LAX an hour late and now all this circling. Third, no I will not put them back. What are you going to do, an emergency landing? Great! Be my guest."

She shrugged and went back to her seat.

We moved into a house that Bob's sister owned in the Latino neighborhood on the east side of Dallas. Our neighbors were great and brought us tamales and tortillas, though in the background I could hear gunshots. Very lively. Right away, I went into a mild depression. I hated the weather and the shop would not be ready for six months. Coming from California, where "anything goes," Dallas just felt so Middle America. The Jews lived in the north, the Mexicans east, the White Trash west and the Blacks south. The chosen ones lived in the middle. That was over 28 years ago. Since then, Dallas has become very cosmopolitan.

My depression got worse and I began to eat, and eat, and eat. Maybe because there was nothing else to do. Maybe it was because I was freezing, and everything was cold and grey like Belgium. One morning I looked in the mirror and realized I had gained twenty pounds with all that fried food and those "Hurricane" drinks. I moved from Brussels to the States weighing 115 pounds and at that point, I was 135. At that moment, I decided to have this new procedure called liposuction. I made the arrangements and flew back to Los Angeles to see Dr. Genender for what he called "a full body lipo." Back then, it was not a pleasant experience, it felt like a huge vacuum that was stuck inside your body. I trusted the doctor, but liposuction was a brand-new treatment and it was very aggressive. I was put under during pre-op and woke up a few hours later in the recovery room feeling like a truck had run over me. I was in a wheelchair for 3 days. I was black and blue all over and could not move for about a week. My body was tighter, but it felt like it had been through a car accident My friend Danielle took care of me while recuperating.

Losing Mom

May 18, 1990, the José Eber and Jeremy salon was finally opening at 8201 Preston Road, one of the best locations in Dallas.

José was in town and we were planning a huge party. Cathy Prather, my PR person, got a local four-girl country band to play outside the salon to welcome the guests, while a DJ would be spinning inside. The band had been playing around at the local bars. I gave them free haircuts in exchange for singing at the party. They were called, "The Dixie Chicks."

The day before the party I received a message from my sister Benedicte. All she had said was, "Please call me; it's important, no matter what time."

I could tell by the tone of her voice that something was wrong. I somehow knew that my mom had just passed away. I called her, my heart beating, my head heavy.

"Yes, you're right, she died just a few hours ago."

"How did it happen?"

"Well, I'd been with her at the hospital the whole day, and I only left for a couple of minutes to grab a cup of coffee. And when I came back she was gone."

While I had known that the end was near it still hit me in the gut. She had been having a series of bad epileptic attacks along with a series of strokes and had been completely paralyzed. All of that at the age of 46.

"The funeral is in three days."

We said our goodbyes and I hung up. I did not even think to call my father.

I knew I could not go to Belgium. I still could not leave the country because I did not have a green card. If I left, they would not let me back in.

The thought hit me hard: *there is no way I can go to my mom's funeral.*

Anyway, I do not think I could have made it in one piece. Yet in a way, I was relieved. I would always be able to remember her the way she was when she visited me. Those would be the last pictures of her in my mind. I cried all evening. Then, while, I was trying to fall asleep, I heard her whisper in my right ear. (Even to this day, I can still hear and feel that moment.) It was she. It was so clear. She was saying my name. I opened my eyes, and she said, "Don't worry; everything is going to be okay." Then for no explicable reason, a sense of peace and joy washed over me. I knew that she was right. She was in a better place now, with no more pain and suffering. She was finally at peace.

In the morning, I woke up looking like Shelley Winters on cortisone. I called José and told him I would be over soon to his hotel. When I got there, he opened the door, took one look at me and said, "Oh my God, all that humidity has made you look really puffy." I laughed, and then told him what had happened. I put on a brave face for the afternoon party at the salon. Ironically, it was only a day after my mom's funeral that I received a phone call from the immigration department; my green card was ready in Brussels. I could not believe the timing. I felt like there were no coincidences in life, that everything was planned for us before we arrive on this earth.

I went back home and stayed with Nadine. The first thing we did was a visit to my mother's grave. Benedicte met us there. She was nine months pregnant with her first child. My parents had just bought a house two years prior and my sister wanted me to see it. The house was a total wreck. There was a bucket full of urine next to my father's bed. The smell was horrific. There was a half skeleton of a rat in the kitchen and spider webs in all the corners. My sister told me that it had been a long time since she had been to his house.

"Dad doesn't want me to clean. I just pick up his laundry by the front door and drop it when it's ready."

With mom in the hospital for months, the place was a total chaos.

"Where is he?" I asked.

"He's at the bar right now, do you want to go there?"

"No thank you, I'm not doing that. Just let me know when he comes home, and I will come back."

We came back the next day. My father was sitting in his chair, same as always. We looked around. I did not want to sit down anywhere. Benedicte was carrying the conversation.

"Take anything you want, if you want to remember her." He offered.

I thought about it for a moment.

"Well actually I'd like to have that frame on the wall with the drawing of her when she was five years old."

"Nah, you can have anything but that."

I shrugged and said, "It's that or nothing at all."

My sister chimed in, "Give it to him; just give it to him, Dad."

"No," he said.

"Fine." I turned to my sister, "Let's go, there's no reason to stay any longer."

I said goodbye but as I made my way to the door, he called out, "Okay fine take it."

So, I did, and it has been on my nightstand ever since.

A few days later June 19, 1990, my sister gave birth to her daughter, Lindsay. My mom liked that name. (A son, Tyler, would follow in August 98.) My plane was leaving that day. I was at the hospital with her. My father was there, along with Concetto, and Nadine, who was going to drive me to the airport. Benedicte went into labor. She really wanted to push the baby out, so I could see her before I had to go. However, Miss Lindsay was not in hurry to come out, so I had to leave.

The Dallas salon

I went back to Dallas, now officially a legal immigrant. Next step was obtaining my citizenship. To celebrate, I bought my dream car, a charcoal 560 SL Mercedes convertible. The first few days I drove it, the racism hit me again. There I was, sitting at a traffic light in the city. The car in front of me contained a couple of guys insulting two African American women who were waiting at the bus stop. They were yelling at them, using the "N" word. I thought I was going to have a heart attack.

I hired Margaux, who was a clone of Whoopi Goldberg, as a shampoo assistant. She was fun to be around and was incredibly spiritual as well. Yet I remember clients whispering to me, "You're going to lose clients if you don't fire the black girl."

Some people refused to have their hair washed by her, while others would leave a twenty-five-cent tip and make a comment like, "That's for the black girl."

When I heard that, I gave them back their twenty-five cents and told them, "Keep it; you might need it to do your laundry."

Another incident occurred when my friend Alfonso came to visit, and we took him to a famous Italian place for dinner. We arrived at the restaurant early because they did not take reservations. Bob and I went inside first while Alfonso finished a cigarette. I told the host that there were three of us and she began to escort us to a table in the completely empty restaurant. Then she saw Alfonso and turned to us saying, "I'm sorry but we are completely full tonight." I was confused.

"But there is no one in here. The place is empty."

She persisted. "We are waiting for a big party any minute and it's going to be hours and hours before something opens up."

Bob and I exchanged looks—we got the message.

I kept remembering the story my grandma told me when I was a kid. "It was a year after your mom was born and it was during the war. We had to escape Belgium," she had said.

"Why?" I asked.

"Because your grandfather's name was Abraham. Although he's not Jewish, somebody in the neighborhood told the Nazis he was, so we escaped to the south East of France in Biarritz and Arcachon and then made our way to Lake Garda in Italy."

After the war, they returned in Belgium.

Maybe I took a lesson from that story or maybe from previous lives, but discrimination is one thing I could not tolerate.

The shop was a big success. I had twenty-five amazingly talented people working for me. Some of them, Christopher, Eric, Jean-Phillip and Sherry had moved from Beverly Hills to work with me. The rest of the crew like Marna, Jesse, Andrew and The Viron Roe came from Dallas. Bob was running the front desk with two receptionists. We made every popular magazine and news channel: D Magazine, Ultra Magazine and the Dallas Morning News. I made friends with Helen Bryant, the gossip columnist for the Dallas Times Herald. Something about the shop or any personalities there was in her column every week.

Anyone with any star power that came through town came to our shop and I styled their hair. I worked with Dixie Carter (aka "Julia Sugarbaker" from the famous "Designing Women" TV series,) Isaac Mizrahi's fashion show, the ladies from the Ross Perot Family, all the local socialites, as well as Hollywood TV personality, Leeza Gibbons.

Leeza was a friend of Cathy, my PR person and she was in Dallas for a big 1960's party at the Texas State Fair. I did her hair, making her look like Pricilla Presley. Leeza, was kind and sweet and still to this day looks fantastic. One day, this young girl came into my shop with someone, I do not remember who, and she made an appointment with me. So, I am doing her hair and the other person is going on about her. "She's fantastic, she's a great singer, and she's going to be so famous…" Blah, blah, blah.

I had never heard of her. *Jessica Simpson, who is that?*

Brenda Vaccaro came to visit her mother who lived in Dallas. She stopped by the salon while I was doing her mom's hair. In Beverly Hills, I used to buy TV Guide every week and circle all the shows I was going to watch. Brenda thought it was hysterical. Behind my back, the first thing she asked Bob was, "Is Jeremy still circling all his shows in TV Guide?"

José would come every month for a few days to do his consultations, as he did in his other shops. New clients would line up at the door; it was a mad house. We would work all day, then go for dinner, and then off to the clubs for the publicity and some fun. The shop did so well that only a couple of months later I was able to buy my first house in the Preston Hollow Estates, the Bel-Air of Dallas. I bought a ranch style home for a good price and redesigned the entire house, adding a pool, hardwood floors and landscaping.

It was now 1991 and my sister Benedicte and her husband, Concetto, and the now 1-year-old Lindsay came to visit us. I hired a limo and went to pick them up at the airport. At that time, you still could pick up people at the gate. They had never met Bob before. I was there with the driver, in uniform, and the three of them came out of the plane gave me a kiss and started to kiss the driver.

I said to Benedicte, "What are you doing?"

"Well, I'm saying hello to Bob."

I laughed so hard.

"Don't you think I could do better than an old man in uniform as a boyfriend?"

They stayed for two weeks. Lindsay was always hungry and her word for food was "Nya-Nya." She used to walk around with food in both hands. Of course, my Gladys and

Dorothy would follow her. They used to grab from the back the food she was holding and scare the heck out of her. Each time, she fell on her butt, started to cry for ten seconds and then say "Nya–Nya." We laughed so hard. To this day, Bob and I still call her Nya–Nya. A year later, I sold the house for a big profit. I wanted to live in a high-rise with a view. I found a condominium on Turtle Creek, one of the prettiest neighborhoods in Dallas, and a few blocks from the famous hotel "The Mansion on Turtle Creek." The top floor of my building housed Greer Garson, the famous actress from the 1940's (of Mrs. Miniver fame.)

Let us travel

One day José called.

"I'm going to Europe for three weeks to shoot a new commercial for my hair products and I want you to come with me. We will be going to Milan, Lake Como, Venice, and Marrakesh."

How could I say no? José, Adam, (his boyfriend), Marcia Riklis (the daughter of Meshulam) from Faberge, and a girl makeup artist formed the team. I was going back to Europe.

I flew Business class to Milan to meet the gang. The makeup girl was also a hairstylist and (it was obvious) was trying to take over my job. I fought her attempts at first, but José looked at me and said, "Listen, the more she does, the less you have to do."

I got it. I left the hair to her. All I had to do was show up in the morning to justify my salary. The rest of the day, José, Adam and I did whatever we wanted.

First thing we had to do in Milan was to select the models. The agency did a casting and we all looked at those gorgeous people parading in front of us with their portfolios. We shot around town for a couple of days. Dinner at night and clubbing after was always on the agenda. Then it was off to Lake Como, the most beautiful place in the world in my eyes. (Gianni Versace had a home there and now it is George Clooney.)

We stayed for three days at the Grand Hotel Villa Serbelloni, built in the 15th century for Marchesino Stanga. It was an old grand palace made into a lavish hotel adorned in gold and velvet and dripping in chandeliers—classic opulent Italian Renaissance style. The Faberge team rented a gorgeous villa not too far from our hotel to film one of the scenes of the publicity. We attended the shoot on the first day and then José wanted to go to Venice. So, the three of us, including Adam, took the train and went to Venice for a long weekend. From the train station, we took a water taxi. After a few turns you entered "the Grand Canal." What a sight! Fantastic, like nothing else, ever. A sparkling city on water. We had reservations at the Danieli Hotel, which was built as a private palace in late 14th century. There was a huge atrium in the center of the hotel. Everything looked like it belonged in a movie. You could not help but think, "Oh my God. The life back then must have been so grand!" I can still see it in my mind today.

We spent a few hours in Murano Island to see how they make art using glass. Amazing, anything you dreamed of sculpted from hot glass. We also went for drinks at the famous Harry's bar. From Venice, José rented a car with a driver, and we went to Florence, which was just a few hours from Venice. We shopped all day, visited the Uffizi, had the most amazing food and then we drove back to Milan to join the rest of the crew.

José then turned to me and said,

"I want to go to Paris to say hello to a good friend. Like to come?"

He was meeting Jacques Morali, the creator and producer of the famous band the Village People and Ritchie Family, to name a few. Unfortunately, Jacques was HIV positive and did not have much longer to live, but our visit with him was one of the best. We went to his condominium in Neuilly, the chicest neighborhood in Paris. He was so funny and all we did was crack jokes nonstop. He was living with his boyfriend who was so good-looking and so nice to boot. Jacques did not seem to care about anything or anybody. Somebody took a picture of us on the Champs- Elysees, and Jacques was wearing shorts. When we got the picture developed, there he was, showing his penis, in all its glory. At night, we went for dinner at Chez Andre, a great restaurant a few blocks off Avenue Montaigne and since then, a favorite of mine.

We stayed at the Hotel Lancaster, built in 1889 and one of the top leading hotels of the world and my favorite of all time. located in one of the most fashionable areas of Paris, the Golden Triangle, of the Champs-Elysees, and walking distance to the Arc de Triomphe, the Petit Palais and the Louvre Museum. José occupied the Marlene Dietrich suite, made famous because she had lived there years ago. After our stay at the Lancaster, it was time to meet the rest of the crew in Marrakech, Morocco. We flew there and took residency at the famous and palatial hotel, La Manounia, facing the Atlas Mountains. Back then, it was the only place to stay. It opened in 1923 and was surrounded by three hundred years old gardens. Winston Churchill used to say, "It is the loveliest spot in the whole world." Ravishing and regal, the Jet Set mingled around the famous pool or wandered the decadent gardens. We dined on Moroccan cuisine while the crew searched for a location in the desert.

We had a few days enjoying the neighborhood and shopping in the Souks, the famous and exotic Moroccan market. The colors and smells were all-vibrant and drew us in every direction, one stall more intriguing than the next. I bought some fabric and rugs, while the locals stared in shock. We were the out-of-place American attraction. Adam and I wore tiny shorts and then, there was José, with his cigarette holder and his hair down the middle of his back. The next day we woke up early to make our way to the desert. The rule there is that you must film before 10:00 am, before the temperature reaches 130 degrees. We escaped to a large tent to hide from the heat and the winds. The desert was both stark and stunning—and proved an amazing backdrop for the shoot.

We found ourselves back at La Mamounia, realizing it was the last day of our trip. We decided to celebrate. I had a glass of Vermouth, and I put in an ice cube. Big mistake. Within an hour, I was experiencing major diarrhea. I could not even stand up. Two staff members from the hotel took me to the hotel's ER, where someone gave me a shot with the biggest needle I had ever seen in my life. I knew I had to rally and quick because my plane was leaving in the morning to go back to Dallas. I was able to hobble my way onto the plane, which was an experience in and of itself. I flew back first class on a Royal Air Maroc. The chef made his way down the aisle and prepared the meal in front of us. I had never seen anything like it.

Getting back to the Dallas routine was a small culture shock. Bob and I went out to dinner every night. However, one of the good things about living in Dallas was that in only 3 hours of flying time, you could be in New York, Miami or Los Angeles. Once a month we would fly somewhere, usually New York where we would stay at the Royalton hotel, dance at either the Roxy, Twilo, Sound Factory, Limelight, The Tunnel, Club USA, The Men's Room or Splash. Sometimes we would have dinner at Chez Josephine on 42nd street. The owner, Jean-Claude was one of the children of the very famous dancer and singer Josephine Baker. We dined while a pianist played Josephine's songs. Then around midnight, the staff would clear the bar, jump on top and start tap dancing—all the while Jean-Claude would sashay from table to table, telling people, "Look what I have to do to sell a bowl of soup!"

A few months later, we decided to take a cruise on the Nile. We flew Lufthansa airlines Dallas to Frankfurt, Germany. The staff kept speaking only German to Bob, who kept insisting that he only spoke English. From Germany, we made our way to Cairo. When we landed at the airport, I was surprised to see so many military around, and especially shocked to see how young they all were. I had made reservations at the Mena House Hotel because I had heard it was close to the pyramids. We were to stay there for three days, and then fly to Aswan to catch the ship. We arrived in Cairo late in the evening, exhausted. The streets were crowded, and everything was dark. I had reserved a suite with a king size bed but when we entered the room we discovered it had two twin beds. I called downstairs to tell the desk clerk and asked him to make the switch.

"I'm sorry sir," he said, "but two men can't sleep in the same bed in this hotel." His voice was firm, clear. I wanted to tell him off. I thought, *I am not sleeping with you, so what is the problem*. However, it was clear he was not budging, and I decided to let it go and chalk it up to their customs. We simply moved the beds together at night and let house-keeping separate them each day.

I woke up the next morning and opened the windows and there, right in front of me, were the Pyramids. What a sight. While it was grand and breathtaking, they were not what I had expected. I had seen pictures and figured that they were all by themselves in the middle of the desert, but in reality, they are next to the packed, loud and cluttered city.

We took a tour and made our way inside one of them. It was extremely hot and humid, and the tunnel was very small. We had to bend over so much that we felt as if we were nearly walking on our knees. Later that day we rode camels. It is somewhat terrifying when you get on them and when you get off—they wobble heavily, and you do not feel sturdy at all. Not to mention the fact that the insides of my thighs were very chapped after that experience. I walked like John Wayne for the rest of the day. Next, we made our way to the famous Cairo museum to see the mummies. The guide had a sense of humor. Knowing that we were Americans, he told us they are saving a space for Cher.

Finally, we made our way to the ship. It was much smaller than I thought it would be. But then again, I discovered that The Nile itself was not that big. We experienced the exact same scenario with the beds—two separate beds in our suite. We started in Aswan, visiting the famous Abu Simbel temples. Then from there, we cruised from city to city making our way first to Luxor (ancient Thebes) where we visited the many grand temples along the Nile River. We went to the Valleys of the King and Queens. We kept imagining what a sight it must had been when they were just finished being built. We would sail at night and go on tours during the day. One evening while we were docked, Bob, who was on the top deck, could hear noise, commotion and whistling coming from the other side of the boat. He went to see what was going on to find out that I was the one causing all the commotions as twenty guys on land were whistling, teasing and making obscene gestures at me. Of course, I was giving it right back to them. The crowd grew louder and louder, with everyone laughing. Bob just looked at me, shook his head and walked away. I could tell what he was thinking: once a slut, always a slut.

It was now time to fly back to Cairo. On the plane I experienced the "small world feeling" when I found Dr. Gary Schwartz, my ex dentist from Beverly Hills seated in the row in front of mine. We were chatting when an announcement came over the loudspeakers, stating that landing would occur in approximately ten minutes. Then suddenly, out of nowhere the plane began to take a nosedive. It dipped so fast, that the people with no seatbelts flew out of their seats. I looked around with horror. Some of them were screaming, some were praying. I noticed a flight attendant had been tossed onto the floor. I looked at Bob—and we shared a glance—as if that moment might be our last. *It was a pleasure knowing you.* We continued that way for what seemed an eternity, heading dangerously close to the ground when suddenly; the plane righted itself and then somehow simply landed so fast that the tail hit the ground a few times. When the plane stopped, the bathroom door opened, and this woman came out of it covered with god knows what. Then the flight attendant stood up, pulled her skirt down, checked her hair, took the microphone and said, "Welcome to Cairo."

Lifestyles of the rich and famous

Back in Dallas, a friend and client of mine, Lori Shaw, was getting married in the South of France. Her mother, Gloria Blackburn, an ex-client from Beverly Hills, was the owner of a few leather couture stores named Jean-Claude Jitrois. Lori ran the shop in Dallas, while Gloria the one in Beverly Hills. She was marrying Jim, a man in the oil business. A three-day event was planned in Saint-Tropez, in the south of France. The rehearsal dinner was going to be an 18th century costume ball. The next day would be the wedding, and the third day a Texas BBQ.

"You have to do my hair for the wedding." she said. "I will fly you over there with Bob."

The invitation was delivered to us at the salon by two valets in full 18th century costumes. One of them performed a drum roll, while the other opened a parchment and declared that we were officially invited to the wedding. You should have seen the people's faces at the shop!

Lori had reserved an entire Mediterranean hotel /chateau, which overlooked the Bay of Saint-Tropez, and she had every guest flown over at her expense. She also had us send our measurements, because when we would arrive in our respective room, our costumes would be waiting. I created both Lori and Gloria's hairstyle. I told her I had an idea for my outfit for the ball.

"Oh really?" She asked, "What is it?"

"Just get me a silver jacket that will cover my butt. I will take care of the rest."

"Okay," she said, "can't wait!" and hung up.

On our way to Saint-Tropez, Bob and I decided to stop in London for four days. We stayed at the Halkin Hotel in Belgravia, one of the most exclusive neighborhoods in London. We shopped at the famous department store, Harrods, and did all the basic tourist stops.

As we traveled, I could not help but think to myself that I loved London. There was a creative energy there I simply could not put my finger on, and it left me wanting to be a part of it. It was not like in Paris, where it feels as if you are a spectator. I felt London was a little more decadent and much more fun and I wanted to be in the mix. We went dancing at my favorite club in the world: "Heaven" located near Charing Cross.

After London, we made our way to Paris to stay at the beautiful and luxurious, Hotel de La Tremoille. Parisian Chic at its finest. The hotel is lined with romantic balconies, filled with marble fireplaces and updated with sleek, modern technology. When I heard that my friend Nadine would be coming to join us I thought, u*h oh, trouble is on its way*.

Having Nadine with me would mean it would not be a quiet visit. We toured the Catacombs, a famous underground city lined with small caverns and tunnels. Housing the remains of over six million people, it has earned its reputation as "The World's Largest Grave." Bones and skulls line the walls and create the archways. At times, you had to crouch down to make your way through a spooky, thin skull-lined hallway. Later, we ate at a charming street bistro and went out clubbing.

After four days of fun, Bob and I flew to Nice, where we rented a car and drove to Saint-Tropez.

The property was fantastic. A couple of stories high, surrounded by beautiful gardens and a tunnel, which took you to a private beach. The Who's Who from Dallas was there. The whole event was being filmed for "the Lifestyles of the Rich and Famous" with Robin Leach.

The night of the costume ball, Lori was dressed like Marie Antoinette, with a beautiful gold and silver gown, and on her head, a big white-haired wig. My costume had less fabric and was far less fancy—a brocade silver jacket with no pants. However, as planned, I wore a pair of silver pantyhose with Prada shoes (with brooches stuck on them) along with a big satin sash tied up in a huge bow around my neck. I hoped no one would think I was a gift.

For make-up, my face was completely made of white powder, my lips and eye shadow were painted a shimmering sliver, and I had black Elizabeth Taylor eyebrows and a black heart as a mole on my cheek. To finish the look, I wore a white wig that I had cut into a pixie style. I looked at myself all done up in the hotel mirror. *DAMN, I looked good.*

Bob, on the other hand, hated his look. He was rolling his eyes at me and my get up while he was putting on a "Mary had a little a little lamb," number with a white curly wig. I did not allow myself to laugh, although, inside, I was dying too.

His shoes were also three sizes too big, curled up at the end with a bell on top. He looked at me in protest.

"I will not wear this stupid costume."

"Bob, you have to—at least for the gala. Everyone will be wearing their outfits."

"Fine, but I will not wear those shoes and look like a court jester!"

We walked down a long stairway until we saw a line filled with guests—all waiting to be announced. There were two announcers, one doing a drum roll, while the other one introduced each guest who arrived.

Drum, drum. "Mr. and Mrs. Blah Blah."

Drum. "Mr. Jeremy Mariage and Mr. Robert Eix."

Bob was red as a tomato, feeling he looked so ridiculous. (I was biting my lips not to laugh.) The look on the guest's faces when they saw my outfit was priceless and Lori absolutely loved it.

It was a sea of costumes. Even the staff was in full costume. It was like a trip to Versailles. Before dinner, all the waiters came out and paraded the amazing French food that was to be served on enormous silver trays. Pheasants, pigs with apples in their mouths, game birds of all kinds, pyramids of fruit, piles of chocolates and cakes—as if we were courtiers in the eighteenth century. We sat down to dinner at elaborately set tables adorned in candlelight. The orchestra members, also in costumes, played classical music as we ate. Then the DJ set up and we danced all night. When the show aired on TV, there I am dancing and twirling around with Lori on the dance floor. Bob never left his chair! Hmm, I am not sure why...

The next day was the wedding ceremony. I designed Lori's wedding dress. It was a mini skirt in front with a voluminous long skirt in the back, all in white of course. Her long blond hair was done up in a French twist, adorned with white roses all the way down the base of her neck. Gorgeous.

My wedding outfit was far tamer. I wore a midnight blue Thierry Mugler tuxedo. The following afternoon, was a barbecue on the beach. Everybody dressed in cowboy boots, hats and fringes. I had been at some amazing events but even this one stood out as a total adventure. Bob and I stayed for two more days so I could show him the Saint–Tropez I used to know and the surrounding neighborhoods. Since then it is Bob's favorite place in the world. Unfortunately, less than a year later, Lori's new husband disappeared. I heard through the grapevine that she found out that he never had money and fled without so much as a goodbye. Rumors were that he ended up homeless in Florida.

A few months later, Bob and I decided to go Aruba for a week in the Caribbean. We dropped Gladys and Dorothy at the canine country club on the way to the airport.

Looking through the windows on the plane, I saw the island and told Bob, "That doesn't look very tropical to me."

I already knew I did not like it. We took a crowded hotel shuttle, and we stopped every few minutes to let people off. After we made a pass around the whole island, and back in front of the airport, we realized that we were the only ones left on the shuttle. The driver asked us what hotel we were staying at—if we could repeat it once more. Turns out it was the first one on the list.

That is how it started. We spent our first hour in "paradise" on that damn bus. We finally arrived to discover that the hotel had individual bungalows situated on the beach. We checked ours only to find out there was huge iguana lying on the bed.

I sighed. *If I am going to have a three way, it sure will not be with an iguana.*

The next day, we made our way around the island. Sadly, it appeared desolated and just plain ugly, upon which I decided that I wanted to leave and go to a different island. I called the airline to find out that there was a flight leaving in an hour to Curacao.

"Book us!" I yelled.

We swiftly checked out of the hotel, rushed to the airport to find it packed to the gills. People in lines were everywhere you looked. Confused workers were processing people slowly and haphazardly. We were not going to make it. I did not know what to do, so I pitched a fit.

"Our plane is leaving soon!" I shouted.

Finally, someone took us to a private office and gave us our tickets. We had ten minutes to get there. The airline representative took us through immigration. We ran like mad, passing hundreds of people waiting in line. We finally got to the front counter, made our way to the head of the line and gave the attendant our tickets. He looked them up and down. "No need, you're on standby."

"What? That is not possible; we just purchased first class tickets with seat assignments. "Look at them!"

"Well sir, unfortunately we are completely sold out."

"So why you are selling tickets if everything is sold out?" I asked.

A man in the middle of the line chimed in, "I've been here for two days trying to get an available seat."

I could see Bob's face growing redder and redder. I feared he would explode any minute.

The airline guy didn't miss a beat.

"Could you please go to the end of the line like everyone else?"

"No, I won't. This is not acceptable. Is there a private plane we can get on?"

"No, sorry."

At that point, Bob had finally had enough, and he let loose. He screamed, yelled, and told the man where he could go and what he could do with himself. That did not go too well. Security ran over to us armed with guns. We were then escorted to a private office where we were bombarded with questions like, "Are you terrorists?"

Yeah, look at my beauty case, I have Chanel grenades inside!

After a while, we realized that we would not be getting off the island, so we decided to stay until our original departure date. Defeated we made our way back to the hotel. It had been about three hours. We dragged ourselves to the counter.

"We want our room back, please."

The woman at the desk shook her head.

"Oh, I'm so sorry; we appear to be completely booked."

"But, but we just left here less than three hours ago!"

"Well, it looks like your room was booked."

"But we paid the whole week, you kept the money. We want our room back."

"I can maybe look into that sir…"

Then Bob exploded once again demanding we get our original booking. She went back to her manager, discussions, paperwork and more paperwork. We got the same room, but we had to pay for another week.

As we made our way to the hotel room Bob turned to me.

"Well, it looks like we may be prisoners on this island. So, let's make the best of it."

We did just that. We drank and shopped all day. Never again, Caribbean!

I cannot believe how much traveling we did in those 3 years living in Dallas.

Leaving José

In every magazine, South Beach in Miami appeared to be going through a major transformation. All the model agencies were moving there, and the city started to revamp the Art Deco district. I told Bob, "Let's go look." So, we headed out for the weekend and we were delighted. The streets were packed with young, half-naked Latinos, gorgeous people everywhere. It was so decadent. The traffic was bumper to bumper, convertibles cars with the music blasting, the retirees on their porches watching like it was a movie. It was perfect, it was still run down, but the energy and sexiness were there and on display. They had one good hotel, The Plaza, one amazing restaurant, The Strand, and two great clubs, Warsaw, and Paragon.

Half of the businesses on Lincoln Road were still abandoned, but I got the sense that Miami was going to explode any minute. On almost every corner, a photographer was taking pictures of a gorgeous model. I knew it when I saw it and I wanted to move there. That afternoon I called José and suggested that we open a shop in Miami. He said that now was not the best time, that he was in the process of selling all the shops and we would make a lot of money. I had heard that story many times. I knew those kind of negotiations could drag on for months, or maybe years or it might not ever happen.

All I could think about was Miami. I knew I was not a good fit for Dallas, yet financially, Dallas was a huge moneymaker. However, I was ready to go and nothing or no one was going to stop me. One of my strength is, when I decide something, I will make this happen no matter what. I called José and told him that I was not happy and that I would move to Miami with or without him. He told me that I would never do it. I was his best asset and he did not want me to go. He asked me to come back to Beverly Hills and begged me to buy Laurent's share of the business—he did not want to be his partner anymore. Apparently, he learned that Laurent's son was stealing from the wallets and the purses of clients. I did not care, once my mind was made up, my mind was made up.

In October 1992, I picked up the phone and called José.

"I'm moving to Miami and I'm leaving the company."

I waited for José to say something, but it was dead silence.

"What? How?" He finally asked. He was clearly shocked.

"I've told you many times that I am not happy, but you never listened. I warned you about my intentions to move to Miami, but you ignored me," I answered.

"How can you do this?"

"Well, Sherry, my artistic director is going to buy me out."

Now José was furious.

"You can't do that."

"I'm done, José. I am ready to move on. Why don't you come out to Dallas and we will have a big goodbye party, like old times?"

He hung up. The following day I received a phone call from José's lawyer. Suddenly it was war. The next step was

138 I JEREMY MARIAGE

a letter stating that the company was going to buy me out, and that Laurent and his wife Fabienne were coming to Dallas to deal with me and take control of the salon. My heart sank as I read the letter. However, I did not know how bad it would get.

Within a week, they came out and took control. No sooner had they taken over than they reported, "There's money missing from the bank account."

Then one of the employees called to tell me that there were rumors going around the Salon that Bob and I stole money.

Please. If I had wanted to steal, I would not have waited until the last day. Idiots!

Since day one, I would divide the net proceeds three ways: Forty-five percent to José, twenty-five to Laurent, and thirty percent to me. I did it the same way every month, including the last month. I had called José many times during that last month, but all I ever heard was that he was, "not available." I think he felt betrayed and took the whole situation very personally. I was hurt, and I am sure he was too. However, life goes on and I did warn him many times of my intentions. In addition, it was not as if I was opening a shop across the street from his. Untangling the whole mess took two months of meetings but finally I was free to go. They made me sign a release contract that said I could not open a salon twenty-five miles from the present location for five years. The contract also included two lists of hairstylists: one I could never hire and another one they did not care about. My lawyer told me to sign and not to worry about it because Texas held a law concerning "the right to work."

Fashion stylists at **JOSE EBER & JEREMY** support the Dallas Symphony and the outstanding works done by its many volunteers. *JEREMY* (in black) is joined by his staff (left to right) *TORRI, ANDREW, JILL, VIRON, BOB, PAM, SHERRY, PAT, CHRIS, MARGOT, BETTY, CHER, JESSE, JENNIFER, MARNA, COURTNEY* and *JEAN-CLAUDE.*

Top: Bob and me at the opening party of the Salon (Mom had just died the day before!) Bottom: The Dallas gang (photo credit unknown)

Top: with Leeza Gibbons (left) and Cathy Prather in Dallas; Bottom:
In Marrakesh with Adam, Jose and friend (personal photo album)

Top: with Cher and Larry North in Dallas (photo credit: J. Allon Hansley); Bottom: with Bob and Dixie Carter at Dallas party (photo credit: Donald Wristen)

Top: with Bob and the Contessa in the South France for the famous wedding (photo credit unknown); Bottom: the two of us in Cairo

With Bob in full regalia for Lori Shawn's wedding in St. Tropez (photo credit: J. Allen Hansley)

CHAPTER SEVEN

Miami

By December 1992, four months after Hurricane Andrew, we finally made our way to Miami. To say it was a total disaster would have been putting it lightly. Oh my God. The town that I saw months before was now completely in shambles. Thousands of houses were destroyed. There were no streetlights. Trees that were hundreds of years old were lying in the middle of the streets. Still, I tried to be positive and move forward. We rented a house in Surfside, in Miami Beach, five blocks from the famous Bal Harbour shopping center. I found a location for my new salon on Miracle Mile in Coral Gables. The location was good, but I knew it would take a lot of hard work to transform the place, which was once a jewelry store. I designed everything, from the stations to the front desk, all of them custom built in exotic red and orange wood. Chairs and lighting were by Philip Stark. A five-foot tall 1960's crystal chandelier was hung in the reception area from an elevator shaft, in front of a Nogushi sofa and table. The floor was concrete. I dipped a broom in gold paint and did some beautiful designs all-over. Deep purple velvet drapes finished the look. Six months and a mere $200,000 later, I was open for business.

The Jeremy salon was gorgeous. No one in town had a place like that. I hired Susan Brussman to work on a publicity campaign and suddenly, I was everywhere. She got me in every publication including Ocean Drive, South Florida magazine, Vogue Espana and the Miami Herald. I was hired to do a makeover on Diane Magnum, the main anchor, and all the hairstyles for the rest of the newscasters of ABC nightly news. One of them, Louis Aguirre, became famous later, for his hosting of Deco Drive on TV and the entertainment show, *The Insider,* in Los Angeles. Suddenly with my name appearing in the credits, the business exploded. People flooded our phones and we were full. I had a highly talented staff of twelve working for me. In addition, as a bonus, being the new hot ticket in town, I found I was invited everywhere, which allowed me to make great connections quickly.

Of course, we had to have a party for the opening of the salon. For the special night, I coiffed Tara Solomon, the queen of Miami Beach Nightlife. She also had a column in the newspaper. I gave her an up-do adorned with palm tree branches and a big pink flamingo and that made the cover of the Miami Herald. She also mentioned my name in her column every week.

South Beach was now the place to be. Beautiful people came from all over the globe to vacation or to re-invent their life. I had never seen so many good-looking people in one place in my life. Hot women and men lined the streets, clubs, restaurants, and beaches. The energy was electric, sexy and fantastic. Bob and I found that we were going out almost every night. I began working with some amazing clients and making unique friendships. One of my more memorable clients was Juanita Castro, Fidel's sister. She truly is a lovely woman and still my client to this day. Moreover, when her niece Alina, Fidel's daughter, fled Cuba in 1993, the first stop she made in Miami was at my salon for a makeover.

I began working with photographer, Iran Issa-Khan. She had done many covers for Harper's Bazaar over the past years. Together we did some amazing work including working with Miss Universe and a publicity shoot with Paloma Picasso. Iran invited Bob and I to a dinner at Barton G restaurant in honor of Debbie Harry (who was a brunette back then.) Later, I went to Palm Beach for a photo shoot with Kathy Ireland (The woman with the most hair in history and so nice and sweet to boot.) I also did a makeover on Florida Governor, Lawton Chiles.

In October of 1993, the company Clairol asked me to participate in an AIDS charity event called *Color Can Make a Difference.* Twenty-five percent of the proceeds would go to the charity, including the sale of T-shirts and ribbons. Then I heard that the famous hairstylist Oribe would be participating. The whole thing went smoothly and I was so glad I could help. We also made the cover of the newspaper.

My friend Nadine and her son Gregory came to visit for two weeks and I took them everywhere. We first made our way to Vizcaya, a glorious Venetian style estate built in 1916 on Miami's Biscayne Bay, then to the Italian Renaissance Inspired Breakers hotel in Palm Beach and finally the Everglades, a huge, lush national park filled with endangered wild animals and sprawling wetlands. They had a blast.

One weekend, I invited my staff to go to Key West. I rented a house and when we got there, we realized it was the annual "Dykes on Bikes" weekend. It was a sea of lesbians dressed like the Village People, (complete with moustaches and sideburns.) We saw them riding bikes all over the Island. In the evening before we went out, one of the stylists told us that she had brought some acid. We all took a piece, except for Gigi (the salon's facialist and a very dear friend to this day) who had a heart problem. We were on the way to the Copa club and as we walked, Karen, the makeup artist, said, "Hey look, this must be working because I can see a thousand roaches on the ground. They are everywhere!"

We all looked down and saw what she saw: creepy crawly roaches scurrying this way and that—so many that some were making their way up people's legs. We figured we were just tripping when Gigi looked at us and said, "Hey guys I didn't take anything, and I see them too." Well then, the screaming really began. We ran as fast as we could away from the bugs, I cannot remember laughing that hard.

The next week Joan Van Ark called me.

"I'm a judge for the Miss American Pageant in Atlantic City. Can you meet me there?"

Well, I did not have to think twice. I knew how much fun an experience like that could be—and I was right. If you want a fun time, Joan is your girl. She took me to all the parties as her date. People still thought I was Bob Mackie. However, since I was not aging (!), Joan corrected them saying, "No, he's his son." We laughed so hard that entire weekend. When I came back to town Peggy Scott called to check on me. It was nice to be in touch with her.

Summer 1994, Bob and I made our way to our local beach as we did every Sunday and Monday. No sooner had I settled down to relax, when I saw something racing toward my general direction. The sun was glaring but I could make out that it was small with big ears and a tail. Moreover, it was jumping a lot. I started to panic thinking it was some kind of big Florida rat that would attack me, but no, to my surprise, it was a teacup Chihuahua. I had never seen the breed before and suddenly, I had to have one. We made our way home, grabbed a newspaper and located a local breeder in Homestead. That afternoon, we brought home an adorable three-month-old Chihuahua. I named her Bianca because her bark was so high, she reminded me of Bianca Castaphiore, an opera singer in the famous Belgian books "Tintin." She was with us for fourteen years.

Although Miami was a lot of fun, I found it a very difficult city to do business. I was not sure if it was the Latin influence which people called, "the mañana complex." Essentially this means that if you need something done today, it can wait until tomorrow. Nobody wanted to work; they all wanted to go to the beach and party. Which is fine with me, but there is a time to party and a time to work. Nothing was accomplished when you want it, and nobody showed up on time. Anything that can happen now can surely happen "mañana."

That approach to life began to drive Bob and me crazy as we attempted to run the business. I looked around one day realizing that beside a few good workers like Andrew, Gigi and Karen, I was supporting the shop almost all by myself. Some of the staff came and went as they pleased. We also found it difficult that many people refused to speak in English. I felt that America was a wonderful country that took us all in—and so in return we should all learn English. However, some of them did not feel that way at all. To our faces they would say, "This is Cuba."

I felt that if I was paying my taxes in U.S. dollars, I should speak English. If I had wanted to speak Spanish, I would have moved to Spain. One time at Publix, a local grocery store, Bob pick up the last loaf of bread on the shelf when a Cuban woman grabbed it from his hand. Bob grabbed it back and the woman started to scream. The manager came over. After listening to the stories, one in English and one in Spanish, he asked us to leave and requested that we give the bread to the woman. We found we did not exactly fit in. (Thank God Miami is not like that anymore; it is so international now. The new generation is so much more open-minded and hospitable.)

After two years of fighting the Miami culture, we decided to move back to Los Angeles. I put the salon up for sale, and Gigi became the manager. Bob and I moved back to California in late December 1994. When we arrived in Los Angeles, we heard about an offer on the salon. It was a businessperson who wanted to buy it for his wife, Ivana. She was a colorist at Tony & Guy salon in Key Biscayne. Negotiations quickly began, and we agreed on a price. It was decided that I would come back for one week every five weeks to service my clients. To make it easier on the buyer, we agreed on monthly payments for one year. This worked for a month, but the next time I arrived in Miami I was greeted with disaster. The remaining staff complained about the new owner, telling me that she was on drugs all the time, sometimes coming to work completely wasted. I realize they were right when I saw her myself completely out of it. Then she and her husband stopped paying the payments. After three months of not paying, one evening, they walked out of the salon—never to be seen from again. They stole all the furniture and the lighting. My lawyer could not find them either. So much money was lost but I knew we had to make a new life back in California.

With Tara Solomon at the opening of the Miami Salon (photo credit: Peter Portillo);

Top: with Iran ISSA-Khan and Debbie Harry (personal photo album);
Bottom: with Louis Aguirre (personal photo album)

The Woman with the hair, Kathy Ireland – Palm Beach (photo credit: Robert Huntzinger)

CHAPTER EIGHT

Back in La La Land

By New Year's Eve 1994, we moved to a house in West Hollywood, on Flicker Way, in the Birds Streets neighborhood above Sunset Blvd and Doheny Drive. It was full of famous people. Behind my house was Liza Minnelli's home and around the corner lived Jerry Seinfeld, Carol Channing and Cheryl Tiegs. My neighbor across the street was Bruce Roberts, a songwriter famous for his tune "Enough is Enough," sung by Barbra Streisand and Donna Summer. Bruce knew everybody in town. The houses were built on a hill, so our home overlooked Bruce's kitchen and living room. He always had tons of famous friends over. He used to call "The Naked Maid Service," aptly named because men would come clean your house completely naked. Bruce used to give us a ring to let us know to look out the window to see his naked house boy cleaning the chandelier with a Swiffer. That was hysterical! Bruce used to throw great parties. I met interesting people there including famous interior designer, Vincente Wolf, and Cindy Crawford.

One night, Bruce called very late. Bob picked up the phone.

"Bob, could you possibly drive a friend of mine to the Beverly Hills Hotel?"

"Are you mad? It is so late, Bruce. I'm tired."

"Trust me you're going to want to go, you'll love this one."

Bob got dressed and pulled the car up in front of Bruce's house, and who came out? Donna Summer, the queen of disco herself. While he drove, they started making small talk and Donna shared that she did not live in Los Angeles. She lived in Nashville with her husband and daughters. She had wanted a quiet life after the scandal. Bob asked her, "What scandal?"

"The scandal with the gays and AIDS." She said she would never turn her back on them. They had made her. Apparently, some papers wrote that she said, "all gays deserved to die of AIDS and it was God's punishment." Everything was taken out of context. She was blacklisted by gays and the sales of her albums went down to nothing.

I met Liza (with a Z) on my street. She just had hip surgery. Bruce was helping her to walk up to her house and I was outside by my car. He waived at me to come over and help him. She looked at me and said, "What beautiful eyes you have."

Couple of weeks later, the doorbell rang, and Bob made his way to find that it was Liza. "Sorry to disturb you guys, but do you have a copy of my mother's DVD at Carnegie Hall?"

"Umm, I'm sorry. No, we don't have that one."

She grimaced and said, "Just exactly what kind of queens are you? Every gay man has a copy of that!"

Then she laughed and went on her way.

On Sunday afternoons, she used to throw parties at her place with a bunch of famous people. Someone would play the piano and she would sing. It reminded me very much of what I thought her mother's Hollywood life was like.

Another night at 1:00 am, when I was out of town, Bruce called Bob, invited him to a recording studio in Hollywood.

"You're going to love it."

When he arrived at the studio, he found Bruce and Liza sitting on the floor, while someone behind the window was working with all the recording equipment. Liza looked at him and said "Bob, you are just in time. They are about to play my new song!"

The music began, and she rolled around the floor and crawled on her hands and knees as she began to sing to the song. It was like a very awkward private performance and it made Bob a little bit uncomfortable.

When the song was over, she crawled over to where Bob was sitting and asked him, "I want to hear your opinion, what do you think?"

Bob said he thought for a moment and said, "You are dangerous."

"That's it!" She exclaimed. "I want to name the album 'Dangerous."

Then she turned back to Bruce and asked him if it was possible to call the album "Dangerous." Later, the album came out with the title "Gently."

A couple of months later we noticed that shady people began frequenting her home. We did not know if she was doing drugs, but suddenly there were cars who didn't belong to the neighborhood going up and down the street. It was around that time that her picture started to appear in magazines saying that Liza was doing crack. It got so bad, that Bruce told her that if this did not stop he would call the police. So very shortly after, the whole thing stopped, and she moved back to New York.

By the end of 1995, I found out that my property owners were having major financial issues. They had just bought a house a few streets over from us, and now, with a bad economy, they found they could not afford two mortgages. Tracy, the wife, decided to sell the house we were renting and made us an offer. They had bought it for $700,000, owed $475,000, and wanted me to take over the mortgage with no down payment. I felt that it was a great deal, but I was a little skeptical because it was still a lot of money. I was not sure what to do. Little Dana Asher, one of my clients, gave me the name of a psychic in Sedona who communicated with spirits and did readings over the phone. I called her to schedule an appointment for the following week.

When that day came, I had just finished my treadmill workout and my right knee was hurting, so I got in bed with my dog Dorothy and called the psychic.

She said a prayer first, then began right out the gate with, "I can feel that your right knee is hurting. And who is Dorothy? And who's Bob?"

I felt like I was on camera, but this woman knew nothing about me. She asked if she could continue and I agreed. She went on.

"I'm now in contact with your mother, she is with a woman with white hair and her name sounds like Ouise-Ouise (her mother Marie-Louise!) She is showing me that something happened to the side of her head. She was not ready to leave this world and she fought until the last minute.

It was very hard for her to go. She is now on the other side and her job is to help people who are not ready to cross over. Her goal on earth was to help you to be right where you are right now."

I listened intently—the space in the room feeling calm and serene.

She continued. "Everything that happened when you were growing up happened so that you would leave home as soon as possible and be able to shape your life the way you wanted it, the way it is now."

I was almost in tears. I missed my mother and wanted to hear more. She continued telling me that my mother had forgiven my father and that I should do the same. She also shared that she is very happy that Bob is in my life because she was afraid I would be alone. At that point, I was crying so badly I could barely talk. At the end of the conversation, the psychic told me to buy the house and not worry about it. Therefore, two weeks later, I did.

More stars

By 1996. I was working at Aida Thibiant, the best spa in Beverly Hills, on Canon Drive. Anna was the colorist and I was the only stylist there, so clients came easily to me. I was friends with Dina, one of the many talented estheticians, who kept me laughing with her stories. She told me that she had to wear a mask to cover her nose when Rod Stewart came in for a treatment because of his severe body odor. The more we got to know each other the more all of us would share stories until we would be cracking up on the floor.

Eve, the waxing queen, was also not shy about sharing some stories. I will spare you the details on that one!

In no time, I was styling Bette Midler, who was extremely reserved. I was a little disappointed, because I was a big fan, but I also know the business and I know that no one can be "on" 24 hours a day. Maybe that is why she is a great actress. Her hair was frizzy and difficult. After I finished I knew she was pleased because she asked me how much I charged for house calls. I told her it was $50 at the shop and $100 at her house. Watching her face drop, I realized that I would not get the deal.

Next, I styled Annette Bening. Annette was all smiles. Her hair was very straight. It made me realize that whoever did her hair for galas or awards shows did wonders. I also got the chance to work with Cathy Moriarty, who was so spectacular in the movie *Raging Bull* with Robert de Niro, and hysterical in *Soapdish*. She was incredibly charming and funny and had a ton of hair.

Another time, I was scheduled with Janice Dickinson, "the first claimed Supermodel," whom I loved. I used to collect her pictures from all the fashion magazines in the 70's. After her massage, she walked in the spa completely naked under her robe, which was wide open. What was great about her was that she clearly did not give a crap what people would say. Her body was gorgeous, but she looked and sounded like she was a little bit out of it. She was hysterical.

"Don't you love my tits? Sylvester Stallone bought them for me."

We laughed through the blow dry. She said, "You're fabulous."

I replied, "No, you're fabulous!"

She said, "You have the best hair."

I said, "No, you have the best hair."

She also showed me her enormous diamond ring. Later, Dina told me that Janice showed her how to get jewelry by teaching her how to give a blowjob. She had demonstrated it on a water bottle.

The months filled with stars continued. It was now Cindy Crawford. I reminded her that I had met her at Bruce's and that I was his neighbor. I asked if she would like a blow dry after her treatment. I was happy to do it. She had fantastic hair. She was a very smart girl (obviously) and spent the bulk of the time asking me about my life.

I went to cut Don Johnson's hair at his house in the Beverly Hills canyons. Don was such a nice man—very charming and much better looking in person, very similar to George Clooney. I always thought that Clooney was ok on TV until I saw him face to face and realized that he was more than okay.

The following months I worked on Candice Bergen, Alicia Silverstone, Patricia Arquette, Claire Danes and Alexandra Von Furstenberg. The funniest of all the women I worked on were the Tweed sisters, Shannon and Tracy. When they were together, I could not even work. I was on the floor laughing so hard. Shannon was an actress and a Playboy centerfold in November 1981 and Playmate of the year in 1982, and Gene Simmons' girlfriend. Tracy was the biggest clown ever. They were like Laurel and Hardy, or Ethel and Lucy. Fiona Copeland used to come regularly and introduced me to her husband Stewart (of the "Police" rock band) and I started to go monthly to their house to cut his hair.

Meanwhile, Bob was the manager of the Art Luna salon. Art was the top hair stylist in the country at that time. He was in every major magazine. The shop, a bungalow with a pretty garden, was located on Keith Avenue in West Hollywood. Some people got their hair done in the garden. Regular folks and celebrities alike were fighting to get an appointment. It seemed that money was no object.

Art used to host fabulous parties to keep all the magazine editors happy. Art's gift was to be the biggest bullshitter you could imagine. He loved to lavish gifts upon important, well-connected people so that they would write about him and keep coming back (very smart.) You were always welcome, as long as you were useful to him. However, the minute he did not need you, you were history. That in fact, became Bob's job. Bob had to tell people they were no longer welcome at the salon. Bob even had to turn down Angelina Jolie, because Art thought she was not famous enough for him. *Who is sorry now?*

Some of Art's regular clients were Angelica Huston, Sharon Stone, Reese Witherspoon, Lauren Hutton, Renee Zellweger, Rita Wilson, Ellen DeGeneres, Michelle Pfeiffer, Amy Pascal, Susan Harris, James Caan, Don Johnson, Courtney Love, Jerry Goldsmith, Diane Lane, Jamie Tish, Eve Quaid, Sofia Coppola, Lisa Eisner, and Patricia Arquette.

Art would go into rages occasionally. Sometimes he would rail against the staff. Sometimes he would take the hedge trimmers, go, and destroy the garden. *Hello Joan Crawford!*

Eve Quaid, Randy's wife, was a close second to Sharon Stone for being the worst customer ever. She never wanted to pay, and she would make everyone leave the salon. She had to have her hair cut in complete isolation. She was miserable, disregarding appointments and often demanding a free lunch. She expected that everyone took care of her needs immediately, right down to Guillermo, the gardener. She used to order him to go behind Art's back and cut flowers for her, so she could take them home. Because of her reputation of being vulgar and hateful, Bob gave her the nickname "Evil Quaid." Art thought this was hilarious and would sometimes call her that to her face, which she seemed to like. Right when it came time for her bill, it seemed that she never had any money on her. One excuse after another. It was later gossiped around Beverly Hills that Randy and Evil were broke.

Sharon Stone was Bob's most dreaded client. "I think she's the most terrible human being that I had ever met," he always said.

Once, Art's assistant was too busy to confirm the next day's appointments, so it was up to Bob to call them. He called the number that was in the schedule book for Sharon. Bob assumed that he would reach Sharon's sister. At that time, she was Sharon's assistant and handled all her appointments. Sharon answered the phone and Bob started to say who he was and why he was calling but was immediately stopped when she flew into a rage and told him to shut up and listen to her.

"First of all, I want to know how the FUCK you got this number?"

He attempted to answer but she cut him off.

"Just fucking shut up and listen."

Bob just sat there and listened to her.

"You are never, ever to call this number again. You are an idiot for even thinking that you could call my private number because I do not talk to 'hired help.'"

While she continued her rampage, Art poked his nose in to ask Bob what was going on because he could hear how loud she was yelling on the phone.

Bob whispered to Art, "It's Sharon. I really cannot take it any longer. I'm going to give it to her when it is my turn to talk."

Art just smiled – he loved confrontation. Finally, she finished yelling, and then politely said, "Okay, so who are you and why are you calling?"

"My name is Bob and I'm calling from Art Luna salon. The reason I called on this number is that this is the number your assistant gave us to call when confirming your appointments."

She started to chime in, but Bob was not having it.

"Just shut the fuck up and listen! Because it is my turn to speak," he said. "Are you available to confirm your appointment for 1 pm tomorrow?"

"Yeah."

"Great. Have a nice day." Then he hung up.

Sharon was another customer that did not think she had to pay her bills. In fact, on her way out she used to yell, "Send the bill to my sister."

Even though some bills never were paid, it was still good for business that she was a customer. Art worked out a deal with her that he would not charge her for services if she came into the salon, but if he had to make a house call, she would need to pay. He called her house, "The Beaver Dam."

A few weeks later Sharon herself called from Napa, California. She was on set filming the movie "Sphere" with Dustin Hoffman and needed her hair color done even though it had only been two weeks since her last color. Bob put her on hold and turned to Art.

"What do you want me to say?"

"I don't know, just come up with an excuse why I can't go to Napa."

Bob paused, collected himself and got back on the phone.

"Unfortunately, Ms. Stone, the total would be about $5000 for Art's plane ticket, limo ride from the San Francisco Airport to Napa and the color touch up."

They both smiled, thinking she would turn it down seeing, as she hated to pay.

"No problem," she said.

So, that weekend, Art flew to San Francisco, took a stretch limo to Napa and knocked on her door. And much like her alter ego might have done, Art told Bob that she answered the door completely nude and she started laughing, thinking that it was funny.

"You might want to at least put a robe on before we start your color," he said.

"I need you to run a few lines from the script with me before anything else, because I need to rehearse for tomorrow's shooting," she said.

"Sharon, I really don't have the time," Art answered. "I'm scheduled on the last flight back to Los Angeles and don't want to miss it."

Art said she got very upset.

"I'm paying you for your time and I will use it anyway I want it."

Finally, Art finished the job and asked for payment. She handed him the production company's card and said, "Send the bill to them, they are expecting it."

On the following Tuesday when Bob got to work, Art gave him the card and filled him in on all the details of his trip. Bob sent the bill to the company. A few weeks later,

Bob got a call from an annoyed man at the accounts payable department of the production company.

"Yes, we are wondering about this outrageous bill for hair color for Ms. Stone. Whom did you speak to and who authorized it?"

"Actually, Sharon gave us your card and said to send you the bill."

"Yeah well, that's not how it works. Only the production company can authorize charges for Ms. Stone. We are not paying this bill."

Bob sent the bill out to Sharon's house. Bob and Art never heard from Sharon again. Art said that was worth losing the five grand just to get rid of her.

Jennifer Tilly was another frequent client of Art's. Bob said that she is just as funny and sweet in person as she was on screen. Once Art went to her home to style her hair for a magazine shoot. As usual, Art was given credit in the magazine for having styled her hair.

About six months later, Bob received some mail at the salon addressed to Jennifer Tilly in care of the Art Luna Salon. The return address was a prison in Arizona. When Bob showed Art the envelope, he told Bob to open it. Bob opened the envelope to find an eight-page hand-written letter to Jennifer from a prisoner. He first explained that he had seen her in a magazine and saw that Art Luna had done her hair and that this was the only way he could see getting her the letter. He then went on to explain that he was a huge fan of hers and that he thought she was the most beautiful woman he had ever seen. The next seven pages detailed what he would do with her sexually if and when he got out of prison. Bob said it was so graphic that it was like watching a nasty porn movie. Some of it was so scary that Bob assumed he was doing time for rape.

It was that experience that helped Bob understand just a bit of what some celebrities deal with from crazy fans. He could not imagine what would happen to Jennifer if this person ever got out. Art wanted to throw the letter away, but Bob thought it would be best if they forwarded it to Jennifer. Art's publicist was a friend of Jennifer's and he thought she could pass it along to her.

In spring 1996, Nadine and Gregory decided to come to Los Angeles from Brussels and paid us a little visit. We were so happy to see them.

One of Nadine's favorite celebrities of all time was Lauren Hutton. She had fallen in love with her in the movie *American Gigolo*. Lauren was a client of Art and had just recently begun taping her own talk show. Bob remembered that Lauren had a color appointment scheduled for the upcoming Saturday. He wanted to surprise Nadine, so he never mentioned anything about Lauren's appointment. He told her he had to go pick up something and then maybe they could swing by and he could show her the salon. Bob called Lauren the day before to ask her if the drop-in would be okay. She said she would be happy to meet Nadine. When they arrived at the salon, Bob told Nadine to come around the corner, so he could show her where he worked. When Nadine turned the corner, Lauren was in the waiting room, sipping tea. Lauren offered a warm smile, stuck out her hand to Nadine and said, "Hi, you must be Nadine. It's very nice to meet you." Bob looked at Nadine and thought she might faint. She stuck out her hand and tried to say something, but it came out in French. Thank God, Lauren spoke some French. Lauren had even brought a coffee mug from her talk show to give to her as a gift. She was the kind of star that made it all worth it.

A week after our friends went back to dreary Brussels, Bob called me at the spa.

"You must go see this tiny Chihuahua down the street in the pet store."

"NO, ENOUGH DOGS!"

However, he persisted.

"Just go look."

"No, I won't."

And I did not. I knew that if I went in I would end up taking it home. After three weeks of Bob pleading for me to "just look," I went to the pet store and here she was, a two-pound little monster! Of course, I fell in love with her and brought her home. We named her Daisy because my Mom always called my pug (named Gladys) Daisy. Finally, we brought home a "real" Daisy as part of the gang. Four dogs!

1997

Jeremy salon, 407 N. Bedford drive, Beverly Hills, California, 90210.

My neighbor, Edward Welter, owned a tiny salon in Beverly Hills on Bedford Drive and was ready to sell it. It was three hundred and eighty square feet, had three stations, two shampoo bowls, and was wonderfully located on the same street as all the plastic surgeons. After some negotiation, I said, "Perfect, I'll take it!"

I bought the place and began to remodel.

Bob came over to manage the new business. The design was great for such a small place. It was my third one and I realized I was good at it. The space was narrow but long. It had a 20-foot high cathedral ceiling and three stations with mahogany mirrors and black cabinets. The front desk was made of a rich dark walnut wood. The floor had black tiles and the walls were painted white and lined with African masks. Two huge Fiddle Leaf Fig trees at the back of the shop separated the styling section from the shampoo area. Every few months, I changed the artwork, so everything would look fresh.

Bob told me that Cathy Provenzano was the best colorist around town and, after a few meetings, I finally lured her into working at my salon. Edward, the previous owner worked there as well. I hired a PR company and suddenly, I was in Vogue, W magazine. Los Angeles Magazine voted my place the 'best mini hair salon in Los Angeles and Allure called me "in and out in 30 minutes, Jeremy is the speed Demon of hair."

I had never once run into José Eber since I had moved back to town. I did send him a letter explaining how I felt and how much he still meant to me. I explained that life was just too short to hold onto anger. I never got a response, but I know he got it.

One of my first clients at the new salon was Joy Enriquez, a singer who was very hot at the time. I also saw Maud Adams, famous for her roles in the James Bond movies *The Man with the Golden Gun* and *Octopussy*, and the only actress who had been a James Bond girl twice.

Another client was Linda Goldenberg, the producer on the movie *Diabolique* with Sharon Stone and Isabelle Adjani. She used to tell me her many "Sharon" stories. She said there was a scene when Sharon was wearing pantyhose with a seam in the back. That each time they did a take, Sharon changed into new ones. Then she had the bill sent to the production company for $4,000. The crew was also fed up with Sharon's behavior. She was supposed to have a shower scene and had requested Evian water in her shower. So apparently, some of the crew peed in the shower tank.

The first time Wallis Annenberg came to my salon, her chauffeur stopped right in front of it, under a "do not park sign." He got out of the car and removed from the trunk a life size painting of her. They both came to the salon and Wallis said to me "this is exactly how I want my hair done."

I thought, wouldn't it be easier to take a picture of the painting?

Wallis's father, Walter Annenberg was, for a few years, the US Ambassador to the United Kingdom. He and his wife owned the famous 200 acres "Sunnylands Estate" in Rancho Mirage, California,

The Estate was a place where the Annenbergs received Presidents like Eisenhower, Nixon, Reagan, Clinton, Obama and the Queen of England.

The year Woody Harrelson was nominated for best actor in the movie *The People vs. Larry Flint* I went to his house to give him a trim before he left for the Oscars. The house was in the Canyon. You should have seen my face when I entered his house. A few disheveled barefoot people were there, including his girlfriend at the time. Woody was running late and was not there yet. The furniture was yellow-stained and there were huge spider webs in every corner. The kitchen looked like a scene from the Disney movie, *The Sorcerer's Apprentice*. Piles of dishes filled the kitchen and were glued to each other with old, dried crusty food. They asked me to sit down, but I declined. His limo was already there, waiting outside, ready to go. When Woody arrived, he ran past us and into the bathroom to take a shower. A few minutes later, he came out with just a towel around his waist, with his big ding-dong flopping around, and sat on a chair all ready for me to cut his hair. Very nice person by the way. When I was finished, someone gave me an address to send the bill, which I did the day after, but they never paid.

I remember once, Bob was standing outside the salon and this girl walked past with her dog. They said hello to each other, and Bob commented that she looked familiar and asked, "Do you work around here?"

"No," she answered.

"What's your name?"

"Renee. What's yours?"

"I'm Bob."

They shook hands.

"So, what do you do, Renee?"

"I'm an actress."

They finally derived a conclusion realizing they knew each other from the Art Luna salon.

Meanwhile inside the salon Cathy and I were freaking out that Bob was just so casually talking to Renee Zellweger! A couple of years later when we lived in Austin, Texas, Bob and I were outside a restaurant, waiting for our car, and this girl came out to pick up hers.

She and Bob looked at each other, and they both said, "Bob?"

"Renee?"

A small world indeed!

The summer of 1997, we went on vacation in the south of France. We flew to Paris first and stayed a few days at hotel D'Aubusson, a 17th century private mansion turned into a boutique hotel on rue Dauphine in the 6th arrondisse-ment, in the heart of Saint–Germaine des Pres. A few blocks away is the famous café de Flore where they have THE best hot chocolate in the world. Nadine traveled from Brussels to visit us. As usual, we were trouble. We took the train and spent the day in Versailles.

A couple of days later, after she had left, Bob and I flew to Nice and rented a car to drive to Monaco. I had rented a condominium almost in front of the Palace. We went to Cannes, Nice, Menton, Cap Ferrat where, at Hotel du Cap, we had lunch in one of the most beautiful settings in the world. We also had dinner in the village of Eze, way up in the mountains, where the view is breathtaking. We then drove down, taking the road where Princess Grace was killed. Bob was driving and trying to look at the view and I was scared to death, trying not to pee in my pants. We also went shopping in Italy in San Remo.

Then we hit the famous (first Tuesday of the month) mar-ket of Ventimiglia, where you can buy copies of designer good and also some stolen real ones like Gucci, Prada, Ver-sace, Hermes.

One afternoon, in Monaco, we went shopping at the clothing store, Replay. In one of the aisles, a girl was bend-ing over looking at jeans. Bob wanted to pass, but the aisle was too narrow, so he waited, but she would not move. I looked at her and I realized that it was Princess Stephanie. Too late, Bob squeezed by and gave her a little push. She almost stumbled over, and Bob said, "Oh I'm so sorry."

Princess Stephanie turned around and said with a big smile, "Oh, don't worry about it."

I learned later that she was the owner of the store.

Between Beverly Hills and Miami

July 15th, 1997, 8:00 am. I was in Miami to work on my monthly visit there to take care of my ever-faithful clients. I was having breakfast at the News Cafe on Ocean Drive in Miami Beach. I had to be at work at 9:00, so I had exactly thirty minutes to eat and then drive to Coconut Grove. Just as I was leaving, there was Gianni Versace looking at magazines. By the time I got to the salon, my 9:00 am client asked me, "Did you hear what just happened?"

"What do you mean?"

"Versace was just killed."

"Are you kidding me?" I was stunned.

From that minute on there was nothing but Versace news—everywhere.

The whole town was dead. Literally. Everybody stayed home scared that Andrew Cunanan might be out to kill them. The restaurants and clubs were completely empty. There was a 24/7 manhunt on for the killer and the police were looking everywhere. What a week. Moreover, strangely with his death, South Beach sort of died too. The glamour was just gone. The fashion crowd left to shoot elsewhere, and South Beach became just another bad tourist attraction. Lincoln Road became a shopping mall. It was never the same.

By the end of that year, I decided to sell the house on Flicker and move a few streets over, on Rising Glen Road, which was above Sunset Plaza. I bought a house that used to belong to Lily Tomlin, a ranch style that I redid into a more mid-century style, adding a pool, hardwood floors, and new landscaping. My first night sleeping there, we did not have any drapes in the bedroom, so during the night we woke up because our dogs were getting nervous. We looked out the window and saw pairs of eyes looking back at us. It was a bunch of coyotes staring inside the bedroom. The morning after we realized that my backyard, almost an acre, was built like terraces on the hills and was the trail for coyotes. That day, I called a company who installed a ten-foot tall fence all around the propriety. However, every night, you could hear them howling around to attract dogs, cats or any small animals and then kill and eat them. Once, Bob went to pick up the mail and he felt something behind him. He turned around slowly to discover that one coyote was four feet in front of him. Nevertheless, that neighborhood was great. Up the street was Britney Spears, next door was Sandra Bullock and on the other side of the street was Justin Timberlake. Jennifer Aniston and Brad Pitt were one street over. When Jennifer was engaged to Brad, her driving skills went out the window. She paid more attention to the ring, than the road. A couple of times, she almost ran into Bob's car, but waved and smiled and said sorry.

We used to go to Sherman Oaks to Casa Vega, a very popular Mexican restaurant, where you must wait for a table, no matter who you are. One evening, after giving our name, we waited in the lobby next to a young couple. Of course, I recognized them right away. Brad was right next to me, in jeans, t-shirt and a baseball cap. Jennifer had been on TV earlier after the announcement that the cast of friends would now be getting $1,000,000 per episode. I guess they were there with a few friends to celebrate the deal. Bob was right next to Jennifer and had no clue. I was trying to tell him softly without making too much of a fuss. We ended up at a table right across from their booth. Jennifer got so drunk that Brad and a friend had to hold her up to get her outside. She was so lucky that there were no paparazzi. Another time, we saw her at Marix, another Mexican restaurant in West Hollywood, also looking tipsy. I guess, like us, she loved those margaritas.

Another time at Casa Vega, we were seated at a table next to Debbie Row, the mother of Michael Jackson's children. She was complaining to a friend that the prior month, Michael's "people" told her to keep all of her spending receipts. She said that she just received a call that this month she was told to shred all of them. Such a problem.

Spring 1998—the accident

I left my hotel by 4:30 am as my plane was leaving for Los Angeles at 6:30 am. I drove my rental car two blocks and approached the yellow traffic light. I drove very slowly into the intersection when suddenly this car came flying through it the from my left and hit me so hard that the car began to spin and then rolled over. Then the airbags exploded. It all happened so fast. The next thing I knew I was lying sideways in my badly smoking car and some people were talking to me, trying to get me out. I remember thinking that the car might explode at any moment.

I was in serious pain. My body hurt from head to toe. My head was pulsing, my arms were sore, and my hands were burned by the airbags. They helped me out of the car safely and I went to the hospital for x-rays. Thank God, nothing was broken. The only issue was that I could not work for a few days because of the burns.

A few weeks later I noticed that I was feeling very tired. I could not move. I dragged myself to ten different doctors, but no one could find anything wrong. They told me it was all in my head. Almost a year later I had already spent close to ten thousand on medical bills and had no choice but to sue the driver who hit me, but Florida has a $10K limit on payouts.

At least, my bills were paid. My fatigue got worse. Some days I could not get out of bed to go to work. This was extremely odd for me—somebody who would go to work on his knees if he had to. However, I just could not move at all. Then I noticed that my stomach began to get bigger and bloated. I just wanted to sleep all the time, but I could not because I found it too painful.

A friend sent me to Dr. Khalsa in Beverly Hills whose practice was across the street from my salon. He was well known around town as, "The herbalist guru." After twenty minutes of tests, he sat me down.

"Well it looks like you have fibromyalgia and a leaky gut syndrome."

I started to cry but this time it was with relief. Finally, someone did not think I was crazy. He put me on a strict regimen for the gut. No wheat, gluten or dairy, and about eighty herbal supplements a day. My stomach went down. The fibromyalgia never went away. I still have it. Some days are better than others and I always experience some form of muscle pain. I just learned to live with it. However, when you see what is going on around the world, I should not complain.

Nadine came to spend the turn of the millennium with us. (Remember Y2K?) One afternoon we went to Pavilions, the grocery store in West Hollywood and we spotted Joan Collins, in full regalia, in an aisle pushing a shopping cart with a half dead plant in it. She was at the meat section looking for sausages. Nadine, who had been a big fan of hers since Dynasty, wanted her autograph. Bob said, "Let me take care of it."

She gave him a pen and a notebook and Bob went to Joan and said, "Excuse me Ms. Collins, I know you're very busy and I'm so sorry to disturb you. My friend is here from Belgium and is a huge fan of yours. Would you mind signing her book?"

She kept looking for the sausages as she replied, "Sorry, I really don't have time. I just got in from Europe and my car is waiting outside for me and this is not a good time."

She went on and on why she did not have the time to sign the notebook. Bob turned to Nadine who was almost in tears, so he insisted.

"Listen, Miss Collins, it's taking longer for you to tell me that story than it would for you to just sign the book."

Without looking, she scribbled something in it.

Well, thank you very much and I hope you enjoy your dead plant and sausages!

A week later, we were back in the same store. This time Bob spotted Faye Dunaway shopping in the produce section. She was wearing a warm- up suit and talking to herself, "bananas, bananas, bananas I need some bananas!"

Someone crossed in front of her and she said, "Get the fuck out of my way, I need my bananas!"

We saw her outside and she began yelling again, "My car, where the fuck is my car!"

178 | JEREMY MARIAGE

A very sweet woman recognized her and walked up to her and said, "Ms. Dunaway, I'll help you find your car. What kind is it and I'll help look."

Faye turned around and yelled at the woman, "Do I look like I need help? I can find my own fucking car!"

I guess when she asked to be called "Mommie Dearest," she really meant it. After finding her car, it turned out to be an old beat up Volvo with one of the headlights hanging by a wire, she stormed out of the parking lot like a mad woman. A stylist once told me that she was hired by Faye to help her choose some clothes because she had just been signed to do the play, "Sunset Boulevard" on Broadway. (We saw her later on in "Master Class," playing Maria Callas and she was phenomenal.) Faye was living in a small bungalow behind The Beverly Center in West Hollywood. After two days, the stylist quit. She could not take all the craziness. Bob used to see Faye at the gym on a treadmill with a Lucite magazine holder on the machine. One time she brought in some nail polish and wrote on the holder, "This belongs to Faye Dunaway."

Raquel Welch also belonged to that gym. Bob and his trainer would be working out and Raquel would walk up to them and lower her sunglasses and say, "Hello Boys." Her trainer had an assistant that used to pass the weights to the trainer and then the trainer would pass the weights to Raquel and Raquel back to the trainer and him to the assistant. Quite a scene. So Hollywood.

The same stylist, who almost worked with Faye, once told me that she was with Farrah Fawcett in New York for that infamous guest appearance on the David Letterman show when she looked completely out of her mind. They were there a few days before the show and said that Farrah must have been on something because she was completely out of it. She never left her hotel room. Two nights before the show, Farrah called the stylist in the middle of the night wanting to talk about clothing. So, she went up to Farrah's room and Farrah opened the door part way. She said that Farrah looked like a complete mess and told her that she was not ready, and to wait outside in the hallway. She waited and waited. It took so long that she sat on the floor and fell asleep. She woke up early in the morning and went back to her room taking all the clothes that she had brought with her. She took the first flight back to California. Later that day she got a call from Farrah telling her that she was ready to see the clothing.

"Well that's not going to work because right now I'm in Beverly Hills having dinner with friends."

She hung up the phone. Well, everyone experienced her state of mind later that week on Letterman!

A few weeks later Bob and I were having dinner at Indochine on Beverly Boulevard in West Hollywood. In the corner booth next to us was Diana Ross and Suzanne de Passe (ex-President of Motown Productions.) It was obvious they were having a great time as the drinks flowed, one after another. The waiter then brought a huge bottle of tequila compliments of a man at the bar. They finished that entire bottle and carried each other out the door.

During this time, I was seeing a lot of Peggy Scott. She and Dr. H. were now living in Beverly Hills, not far from Sunset Boulevard, just two minutes from my house. The house resembled a New England cottage, with a shingled roof, all decorated with white trim. Peggy told me that she had worked on the design with the famous interior designer Barbara Barry. You entered a small foyer. On the right was the kitchen, followed by the housekeepers' quarters and the laundry room. On the left was a hallway with Dr. H.'s home office and the master bedroom complete with his and hers bathroom and closets. Upstairs were two bedrooms that she used as storage. She would later build an office next to the gym in the back of the garden, behind the pool. At the time, while doing her hair she would say "Hurry up, I'm running late for the office," and I am thinking *but it is just across the pool*. There was a living room, dining room, and TV room overlooking an English garden and pool. It really was the perfect size yard and house. Everything was in proportion and understated. There was nothing pretentious or "in your face" about her decor.

She had two small dogs as well, a poodle who barked all the time, and a Pekinese, who was my best friend. She had German Shepherds that lived outside of the house in the garage. Unfortunately, she did end up killing one herself with a gun. One of them barked at her and she felt unsafe.

She had two housekeepers. Every Sunday night the menu for the next week was printed out so that the cook would know what to prepare for the week. Every night, when in, dinner was served in the TV room. Two tray tables complete with a rose in a vase was set for each of them. Peggy told me that she had a blood disease that makes her extremely weak. She took a lot of supplements and homeopathic remedies. I worked on her hair once or twice a week depending on her schedule and all the photo sessions. She was mostly on time, but occasionally she was late and appeared completely down or wasted. I knew she did not drink so I assumed it was her disease. Having fibromyalgia myself, I knew what it was like to feel and look exhausted. She and her husband really seemed the perfect couple. It was like a movie. Perfect house, perfect marriage, perfect as a picture. Which always brought me back to that thought that it all was just too good to be true.

I remember Bob and I being invited to a tea party at the house. We were both sitting in the garden when this older, tall blond woman came over and started chatting with Bob.

"Well, how do you know Margaret?"

Bob said, "Margaret who?"

"Well my daughter of course, the actress, Peggy"

"Oh sorry! Jeremy does her hair." Bob explained.

She swiftly left the chitchat behind and started complaining about Peggy. Then she had another drink and began babbling about how Peggy had forgotten where she came from and how mean she was to her.

"Peggy acts so grand and fabulous but…"

She went on and on. When Peggy caught a glimpse of Bob talking to her, she rushed over and ushered her mother away.

A few weeks later Peggy started in a new TV series with some other well-known actors. Peggy shared with me once about a co-star's cocaine use, saying that her nose was often crusted over. When I did Peggy's hair for a shooting for Harper's Bazaar magazine, with the cast, I could see that star's nose myself. Not pretty.

**

September 2000, I am turning 40! Should I celebrate or kill myself?

I will always remember, back in Brussels, when Nadine turned 28.

I was 21years old and I looked at her and said, "OMG, you are so old! I think when I reach 30, I will kill myself."

She was completely devastated.

Of course, I was now 10 years overdue and not ready to go, so I decided to celebrate.

Bob and I went to Hawaii and stayed at the Four Seasons on the big island.

Cabo

Las Ventanas Hotel had just opened in Cabo San Lucas. Bob and I went down there for a few days. The property was spectacular. It had a long driveway and in front of the entrance, staff would be there to greet you by name and offer you some refreshments. By the time you turned around, your luggage was already taken to your room. I reserved an upstairs one-bedroom suite with a private terrace and mini pool. That is what a $1,000.00 a night could buy you twenty years ago! Bob spent his days swimming and baking in the sun while I was at the spa having treatments. One evening while we were having dinner in the main restaurant on the terrace when a man walked by.

"That's Bill Gates." I said.

Bob did not believe me.

"That's impossible. The world's richest man would be on a yacht or private villa."

I said, "Trust me, I can recognize people with my eyes closed."

The day after, we were having lunch at the seaside café and two couples sat down at a table next to us.

"I'm telling you, that is Bill Gates."

Bob was about to dispute me when the other man at their table asked, "Bill, do you want to split a bottle of wine?"

Bill replied, "Not at these prices."

He was sitting on his hands, with a small book on his lap—strangely rocking back and forth, as a child might.

His wife Melinda was telling her friends, "I can't believe that after spending millions of dollars remodeling the terminal for private planes, it's still an embarrassment. First you must park your plane so far from the entrance, and then, the furniture in the terminal is awful and the bathroom was atrocious and on top of that, no restroom attendants."

That afternoon we went out for some sun by the pool, me under an umbrella, of course, while Bob was deep-frying. Bill Gates was in the pool with his two-year-old daughter. Some woman noticed them, jumped in with her child, and swam over quickly. Then more and more people were getting in the pool with their kids surrounding Bill and attempting to get his daughter to play with theirs. Melinda got her daughter out of there fast. Bill swam on over to the infinity edge of the pool where Bob was sitting. Just off shore was a beautiful yacht. Bill told Bob, "I've always wanted a boat like that."

Bob found that very funny that he did not have one.

The girls

Since we had moved to the new house on Rising Glen, Dorothy, our Boston terrier, seemed to be disoriented. We took her to the vet and found out that she was actually almost blind. That explained a lot. She must have been going blind in the old house but had just memorized the layout. In the new house, she was completely lost. We decided to get her to a specialist who would implant a new cornea in one eye. She suggested doing the eye that was completely gone in case of complications. Dorothy could see just enough in the other eye. The minute the surgery was finished, it was as if a completely new world opened for Dorothy. She could see everything right away. It looked like she was wandering around saying, "Hey, when did we get these Chihuahua's, and when did we move?"

Unfortunately, soon after she got a tumor and lost her vision once more. We had the other eye done hoping that that time everything would be okay, and it was.

One Saturday night Gladys was taken over by a coughing fit and could not stop, so we took her to the emergency animal hospital. They had to put her in an oxygen cage. On Sunday morning, I left for Miami. On Sunday night, Bob called to tell me that she was not going to make it. I have never cried like that—ever. I was not crying actually, I was sobbing so loud it sounded like I was screaming. She needed to be transported by special ambulance with the oxygen tank to a specialist in west Los Angeles. It turned out that it was Dr. Ettinger, the doctor who wrote "The Book of Veterinarian Medicine."

The diagnosis was that all the small branches in her lungs were collapsing and she was not getting enough oxygen. She became more stable after a week. I was a complete basket case. This was my baby. I remembered how she would wait for me every evening after work greeting me first and then taking me to every room of the house to show me, "Look, this one peed in this room, and this one pooped in this room."

She lasted a few months like that and we realized that she was suffering. As hard as it was, I did not want her to go on suffering. I felt almost as if she was staying alive just to make us happy. One evening, I made a hard decision. I asked the vet to come to the house to put her asleep. What a night that was. I will never, ever forget it. When I finally went to bed that night, I had a dream of her. She was young and happy. She was somewhere with blue skies and green grass, jumping as she used to do, like a gazelle. Bob and I always thought there must have been a little alien inside that body.

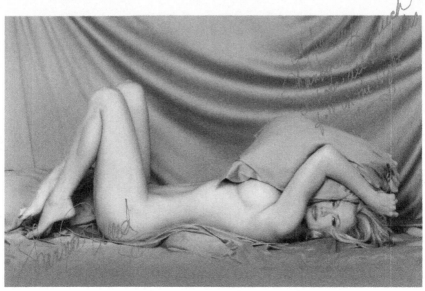

Top: In Hawaii with Bob for my 40th birthday; Bottom: The ever gorgeous and funny Shannon Tweed (photo credit unknown)

flirt perfect
the short cut with sass!

Designed by Jeremy, a shape **master** at Los Angeles' **exclusive** Aida Thibiant Salon,

this crop is **perfect** for anyone, *anytime!*

Here, he **shows off** three of the versatile design's **many** looks—

and tells **you** how to get the cut to make it all **happen!**

▲ the cut

"One haircut, so many different styles," says Jeremy. "And all of them can be done in less than five minutes." Start with a short and feminine design, and it's a cinch. The cut is designed using scissors only, with a bit of texturizing at the ends to add movement and volume. And, if you're worried about how your face shape might affect the look, Jeremy says. "If you have a round face, give the cut a longer neckline and add higher volume. For a (narrow) face, get fuller sides and a shorter neckline."

look fresh

Jeremy lifts at the roots for volume in this style (above). To create it yourself, towel-dry hair and add a thickening spray to the roots only. Using a blow-dryer and your fingers, lift for body as you go. Easy for those busy '97 days!

look fabulous ▲

This sizzling look is ideal for that romantic evening when only the most sophisticated styles will do the trick. Start with damp mane and apply a thickener to roots. With your fingers and wide-tooth comb, sweep hair up and off the face before letting it dry naturally. Or, if you're in a hurry, blow-dry instead, shaping in the same method. Either way, spritz finished look with a shine enhancer and you're ready to glow.

◄ look flirty

On damp or even dry hair (for an instant change!), apply gel to palms and then run through hair. For the best look, try using a dual-action product that gives you hold but ups that shine. Next, simply part low on the side and style into place using a fine tooth comb. To finish, you can spritz on a bit of glossifier and pat hair so that it truly hugs your gorgeous face.

A sample editorial piece of my work. This one is for Sophisticated Hairstyle Guide magazine (Photos by Ladi)

CHAPTER NINE

Spring 2001 - Austin

After a few years back in Los Angeles, I grew weary of the place. There is only so much you can take of the city. My salon was a couple of miles from the house and sometimes the commute would take 45 minutes. I offered Cathy, my colorist, to buy the salon, which she did.

We decided to sell the Rising Glen house and move to Austin, Texas. I wanted to open a home decor store. Doing hair was taking a toll on my body and I felt ready for a change. While the house was on the market, the actor Michael Vartan, (Sylvie Vartan's nephew) from the TV show Alias and the movie *Monster in law*, came to look at it a few times. After the last visit, he made an offer and we accepted. A few days later, Michael stopped by again, this time with his girlfriend. While they were looking, Michael's mother "showed up." It was a little uncomfortable because Michael introduced his girlfriend to his mother right in front of us. She seemed surprised and it was obvious that she was not happy about the situation with the new woman in her son's life. He gave her a tour of the house explaining to her what

190 | JEREMY MARIAGE

his intensions were for each room. The front room that we used as a very large dining room was to be a billiard room. His mother did not seem that impressed with his ideas, never saying a word, just looking on in silent disapproval. On the day of inspection, we were there along with our real estate agent and the inspector. The inspection was supposed to start at 9 am. By 9:15, no one from Michael's team had arrived. At about 9:30, the doorbell rang, and Bob went to open it. It was Michael's girlfriend telling Bob that Michael had changed his mind. He was withdrawing from the deal. It was a big disappointment.

A week later Jane Krakowski, the actress from Ally McBeal, and 30 Rock, came to look at the house. She visited again a week later and wanted to sit and try on all the furniture to see how "comfortable" she felt in the house. An hour later, I had assumed she had already left. I went into the master bedroom to find her lying across the bed.

"Umm, excuse me, but what are you doing in here?" I asked.

"I just wanted to see how I would feel sleeping here, in the bedroom."

I wanted to shout at her, "You damn crazy loony, get the hell out of my bed and my house!" but of course I wanted her to buy the house and so I told her that she could probably get a better feeling if she thought about it in her own bed. A few days later, she came back with friends of hers to the house. She took all of them on a tour. They made their way out to the pool and sat around on the furniture just chit chatting. They sat out there for at least a couple of hours until sunset. Jane came back in the house and asked if she could have a party that night with a few friends. Of course, I said no. The next day, our agent called and said that Jane had made an offer, however it was so ridiculously low. I countered back but we never heard from her again.

Then, on September 11, early in the morning my phone rang. I was still half-asleep.

It was Nadine calling from Brussels.

"Turn your TV on now," she said. "There's a bomb at the World Trade Center. Oh my God!" she screamed. "A plane just crashed into the tower!"

By now, I was awake. I shook Bob and told him, "I think something bad is happening right now in New York."

We both rushed to the living room and turned on the TV to realize (like the rest of the world) that we were experiencing a living nightmare. Of course, we did not go to work that day. No one could keep their eyes off the TV. Up to this day, you cannot help being shocked when watching what happened.

A few weeks later Peggy told me that, she and her husband had to cancel their trip to Israel. She said the government told him he could not go because he was Jewish and that someone warned them of a potential kidnapping threat against Peggy. Apparently, Bin Laden was in love with her and had ordered her to be brought to him. I had to listen with a straight face.

Our house finally sold. A studio executive bought it. He also did some remodeling and sold it later over twice the price to the stylist Rachel Zoe.

On the road again

In December of 2001, we left Los Angeles and drove for three days to Austin, Texas. When I got there, I became very depressed and a couple of months later I had gained 20 pounds. I now realized that Texas is excessively fattening and expensive (another lipo?) for my figure. I was now going to Beverly Hills and Miami every fifth week to work on my clients. I took 80 planes a year just for work. We lived up in the hills in a 6,000-sqft three-story house. It had a spectacular view of Lake Austin. At night, the sunsets were incredible. I would pick up the newspaper in the morning to find a couple of deer eating in my front yard.

Businesswise, I rented a space in Davenport village in the community of Westlake. After a few months of remodeling, I finally opened my design shop called "Now & Zen." I sold gorgeous things for the home and Bob hosted a tea bar. It was a big space and we used to have cocktail parties there. Being new in town, I was also in every magazine. It was a great concept but apparently simply too Avant-Garde for the area.

A year later, my Dorothy began losing weight very fast. It got to where her legs could no longer hold her up. After a few exams, she was diagnosed with Leukemia and we were told that she was probably going to get worse very fast and that eventually she would not be able to walk. A few weeks later, while in Miami, Bob called to let me know that he was going to have to put her to sleep that day.

Bob said that she had come to let him know that she was ready. *No, not another one.* I said my goodbye to her on the phone. Although she was deaf, I am sure she got the message. Poor Bob. Dorothy was his girl and I knew he was going to miss her as much as I was.

Nadine's son, Gregory, wanted to come spend some time with us. Of course, we invited him to stay in our guesthouse.

He stayed for six months, while helping Bob's brother-in-law do construction work.

I sent a plane ticket to Nadine to come for ten days knowing that for her to be separate from Greg would be a challenge.

Top Photo: in Austin, 2001, (left to right) Cisco, Gigi, me, Bob; Bottom photo: (left to right) Bob, Nadine, me, Gregory (personal photos collection)

CHAPTER TEN

Miami Round Two

After two years of boredom in Austin, we closed the shop and decided to move back to Miami, which at that point had become much more international. I rented, close to Midtown, a gorgeous three-bedroom condominium on the 29th floor of the "Grand," a high-rise by the water, on N. Bayshore Drive. It had fantastic views of Biscayne Bay and Miami Beach. It was where Don Johnson lived while filming the TV series Miami Vice. Of course, I continued going back to Beverly Hills every five weeks to take care of my clients.

Soon, I opened a small design store on Fuller Street in Coconut Grove. Bob and I went to all the major home and gift shows. This was also a great excuse to travel. We made our way to places like Los Angeles, Manhattan, Atlanta, Dallas and, of course, Paris at the famous Maison and Objet show. Next door to my boutique was M Salon, a very stylish hair salon, which came in very handy. I did my Miami clients every five weeks there, and the rest of the time Bob and I were next door at the boutique. Michael, the owner of the salon happily sent over all his clients and we were ecstatic because Miami was booming. They were building condominiums so fast it felt like they were popping up overnight.

Then in the blink of an eye, there were three hurricanes in a row. The worst one, Katrina, came to Miami in August 2005.

I remembered telling Bob, "Listen, we have a lot of artwork on the wall so let's take them down now."

"No," Bob answered. "It's going to bypass us."

Well of course, at 2 am Bob came to the bedroom to wake me up.

"Hurry up its coming straight for us; we have to remove all the art."

"Thank you very much mister."

In fifteen minutes, we rushed to move everything into the bathroom where, with my two Chihuahuas and a radio, we went to hide. The wind was already out of control. There was a high-rise building being built next to us and the crane on top was spinning like a helicopter. We started to feel this strange motion and then realized the building was swaying with the wind. We felt like we were at sea. We heard a loud explosion coming from inside our building and Bob went out the front door to check it out.

All the condominiums are enclosed and around this atrium that goes from the first floor all the way up to the 42nd floor, topped with a glass ceiling. That sound we heard was one of the glass sections exploding in and falling 42 stories down to the fountains on the first floor. One side of our building also had a wall of glass that looked out over the city, those glass sections started to implode into the atrium as well, and it created a vacuum in the building. Bob came back inside and could not close the door because of the suction from the atrium. We both had to get on the floor with our backs to the door trying to push to close it. Once we did, our patio doors and windows started to bow inward. We just knew we were going to be sucked out.

We moved in our tiny little storage closet huddled together in the dark for hours, not knowing where the storm was and when it would end. Bob finally got a signal on his cell phone and called his mom in Texas so that she would watch TV and give us an update on the storm. Once it had passed, the first thing we did was to go out into the atrium and see what the storm had done. We looked over the railing to the first floor and could not believe what we saw. There was so much debris and glass down there as well as someone's sofa and refrigerator. On the 42nd floor, someone's condo had exploded from the inside out and the vacuum sucked everything from the walls, doors, and furniture inside to the atrium and landed down on the first floor. It was quite a sight!

The entire city was without power and ours did not come back on until a week later. The building's generators had failed during the storm and we had to walk up and down twenty-eight flights of stairs every time we took the dogs out or went to find somewhere that had electricity to get something to eat. It took a huge financial toll on the area and of course on my store and, though we did not want to, we had to close our doors. However, this was nothing compared to those unfortunates in New Orleans.

Since we did not have the boutique anymore, I wanted to travel with Bob, so we went on vacation to Spain. We flew to Madrid then made a connection to Malaga, in southern Spain. We rented a car and drove to the port of Marbella, which I found to be a big disappointment. I had remembered Marbella from the early 80's. Back then, it was the Saint-

Tropez of Spain. So fantastic, so chic, so exclusive. Now it was lined with cheesy McDonald's and Pizza Huts. Busloads of tourists packed the streets. Every restaurant had the menu in 20 different languages. What a dump! However, the travel experience made up for it.

It started in the Miami airport when my two business class tickets, we were upgraded to first because of oversold seats. Then, when we got to the front desk at the famous Marbella Club hotel, although my reservation was for a deluxe king room and because I paid with American Express, we were upgraded to a private villa. We stayed there a few days, lounging by the pool, sipping sangria.

Later, we drove in the country, to Ronda for lunch. Then, we went to Gibraltar to see the monkeys. We got hungry, so we stopped for a quick burger and you should have seen my face when they charged me for each individual packet of ketchup. I realized how spoiled we are in the States.

We flew back to Madrid, staying at the Villa Magna Hotel. They also upgraded us to a beautiful suite. We did the typical tourists circuit, from the famous Prado museum to the Royal Palace. Then of course shopping and dining. We also got an upgrade to first class on the way back.

Months later, we made our way to Buenos Aires. Oh my God, what a fantastic city. I loved it! It had the look of Paris and Madrid with the energy of New York. Traffic lined the big bustling avenues. Yet it would get very quiet the minute you turned a corner. There were parks everywhere and of course, those famous dog walkers, walking ten dogs at the same time. Beautiful people. Great restaurants. I felt I could move there in a minute. Bob loved it too.

I started checking around to see if I could make a living there as a hair stylist but the most expensive haircut in town was $45.00 and I was charging $150.00. We rented a beautiful apartment in Recoleta, the Beverly Hills of Buenos Aires, close by the famous" Recoleta cemetery" where Eva Peron rests with 6,400 aboveground mausoleums. Michael from the Miami salon joined us. I also traveled with my two Chihuahuas. The dogs were a complete success. People stopped us everywhere to look at them. Every day we explored a different neighborhood. We went to La Boca, were all the houses are painted a different color. We took a tour in the famous Teatro Colon, Plaza de Mayo, and strolled in Palermo SoHo. We went to the flea market where, on every corner, couples were dancing the tango. Bob and I have been back there a couple of times and we still love it.

A couple of nights after I got back to Miami, my dog Daisy peed in bed. She had never done that before. She looked scared and dazed. Something was wrong. The next day, she had a seizure. She was not breathing, and I began to panic. Bob performed mouth to mouth on her and finally she came back to life. We rushed her to a specialist and they did some tests. They came back negative. A few months later, she looked weird, and then, suddenly three days later she died of kidney failure. I could not cope. All I could think was . . . *No, no, no, not my little one.*

Bob and I were a complete mess. I sobbed out of control. We drove to the hospital to see her for the last time. She was there with her tongue sticking out. I gave her so many kisses, heartbroken that I would never see her again. I kissed her one last time and whispered to her, "Goodbye my "puce." Which means 'Little flea 'in English, my special name for her.

I only had my other Chihuahua, Bianca, now and that was going to be it. She was the last one from the original "gang" of four. Bianca looked lost and did not want to move or eat. I asked the vet what I could do for her.

She replied, "Might be best for you to get another dog."

"Can't we just give her a happy pill instead?"

"No, she needs to be distracted by something and another dog would do the trick."

The next thing I knew Bob was checking online and there she was. Miss Trouble. A brown Chihuahua named Faith, pictured with a pink boa around her neck. We went to the pet store and that poor thing was there. Nobody had paid any attention to her. She was already six months old and her tail was broken. A chunk of hair was missing on her backside and she had a scar. Her head had been shaved. I am sure she was never walked and was out of shape. We felt that she must have been abused at some time. On the top of that, she was on sale. I took her in my arms and she grabbed me; she was not letting go.

"Bob if we don't take her home they will put her to sleep or send her to the pound."

All the way home we could not stop laughing because she looked exactly like the donkey in Shrek. We brought her home and hoped Bianca would be happy, but she just looked at us with eyes that said, "Another one?"

We could not find a name for her for a week. She was up and down, running everywhere. Peeing everywhere. Being a pest to Bianca. She was so terrible that we named her Muriel (from the movie *Muriel's Wedding*.) There was a scene in the movie where Muriel was being bad, and her sister looked at her and said, "Oh Muriel. You're terrible."

A couple of months later, I wanted to show Amsterdam and Switzerland to Bob. We flew to Zurich and spent a few days there. Then we made our way to Lake Lucerne to spend some peaceful time. Overlooking the serene water, The Seahotel Hermitage was located across the street from the lake and for five days, we relaxed by the water and walked to town for dinner. Then it was on to Paris to a boutique hotel, right behind the Louvre, where our suite, under the roof, occupied the entire floor. My sister Benedicte and her husband Concetto met us there for the day. Finally, we made our way to Amsterdam, which is absolutely one of those fantastic cities. Bob loved it. He wanted to move there as soon as possible. A few days later, we took the train to Brussels to see friends and family. We stayed with Nadine. My siblings, Benedicte and Fabrice, came to visit with their families. We had a huge BBQ in Nadine's garden. We had so much fun, maybe except poor Bob who does not speak French. We had the two dogs with us the entire trip. They were so international.

We had been to Puerto Vallarta a couple of times before and each time we had loved it. The Four Season's in Punta Mita just opened, and the hotel offered a special package. We flew there and we had a car pick us up. We then drove forty-five minutes north of town. We checked in to this fantastic lobby and were showed to our room. I thought it was very comfortable, but looking out at the balcony, I saw that the room a few yards from us had a small private pool. I called down to ask how much to upgrade. They said we could have that junior suite for $100 extra a day, since there were only three other couples in the hotel. Great, I will take it. Ten minutes after we were settled into our new room. I realized that the phones in the room were not working. I went to the front desk and complained. They said they were so sorry, but the three other guests occupied the other same suites. "We are so sorry, but we are going to make your stay very pleasant and we are sending somebody right away to show you your new room." They gave us the biggest waterfront one-bedroom villa with a private pool, as another upgrade. Here's my lucky star again! Bob and I really loved Mexico.

Meanwhile, I continued my work with Peggy whenever and wherever she needed me. I flew to Philadelphia every couple of months to work with her at a television shopping network for her line of cosmetics. A driver would pick me up at the airport and drive me to the hotel, twenty minutes outside town. Peggy always stayed in the only suite, a spacious one bedroom, with a living and dining room and kitchenette. I always had the room next to hers as it had a connecting door between the two rooms. Peggy's make-up artist stayed down the hall. Peggy used to slide little notes underneath my door all the time: "Welcome back honey!" or, just drawings of little hearts.

The first TV segment was usually aired between midnight and 1:00 am. Some people do not sleep, so they shop. The other spots were at 6:00 am and 3:00 pm. We took naps in between. Each time Peggy was on screen we had to do her hair, make-up and clothing. She would order us lunch and dinner and the two of us would sit around watching the TV, munching, talking or gossiping. It was hard work, especially for her, as she had to look and sound good on camera regardless the time of day or night. She was so good at it. She used to sell the crap out of those products. She told me that she would sell about a half of a million dollars' worth of products on her visit there.

Peggy told me that the company kept 50% and the other half was hers, but she had better sell well or they would drop her in a minute if she did not make the expected goal. Her distribution company had to pay to make the cosmetics not to mention the other expenses like shipping, travel, hair, make- up, hotel, cars, etc....

I also worked with Peggy on all her infomercials that were directed by a production company based in San Francisco. The company would rent a house or a studio and then hire a famous guest or some other celebrity. Once, Peggy rented a van and transformed the interior into a facial room. They would drive around the neighborhood and surprise customers, offering them a facial right there in the van. Every month I would receive my products supply by the mail. Peggy was very generous. For Christmas and birthdays, she gave things like Tiffany clocks, Cartier key rings, Hermes cosmetic bags, Hermes china.

Once I was explaining to her that one of my Chihuahuas was to have knee surgery in two weeks and she asked, "How much is this going to cost you?"

"$2,500.00," I answered."

A couple of days later, I was so surprised to find in my mail a check from her for the total amount for the surgery! That is how generous she could be.

The call

November 1, 2006, I received a call from my sister letting me know that my father was in the hospital. It was something with his heart. Jokingly, I was thinking *his heart? He does not have one.* Four days later, she called back.

"Okay I have good news and bad news."

I sighed. "Good news first please."

"Well, Dad is out of the hospital."

"So, what's the bad news?"

"Well, he's dead. The funeral is in two days, are you coming?"

While I was stunned for a minute, I did not need to think about it. I was not going to go. There was not any point. Then I thought about it another minute and I said, "If I come, it would be only to support you and if you really, really wanted me to come, I would be there for you."

Well, surprise! She wanted me to come. I said that if the airline ticket was too expensive, I would not go.

I called the airline and discovered that they had a special price of $300.00 for people who have had recent deaths in the family. I had no excuse now. *Fine, I will go.* Business class was full, so I could not upgrade. I flew from Miami to Chicago, barely making the connection for Brussels. My seat was the last row in the plane and I was the only one sitting there. The flight attendants chitchatted with me right away, since they were behind me with the food and beverage cart.

"Are you going for pleasure or business in Belgium?" One of them asked.

"Well actually, my dad died yesterday and I'm going to his funeral," I said.

"Oh, so sorry for your loss," one of them answered. Usually the last row on the plane is reserved for us in case we want to rest a little bit during the night, that's why nobody is sitting here but here some pillows and blankets, you can have the three seats for yourself, we still have the other side and it's a full flight anyway, so we won't have time to sit down."

They spoiled me for the whole trip. They got me food from first class and champagne (of course I can be very charming when I need to.)

Nadine picked me up at the airport and I stayed with her. I took the train from Brussels to my hometown the following morning. My brother-in-law picked me up at the station and we went to the mortuary, where dad was lying in his open casket, before being cremated. My sister informed me that in Belgium, the family cannot keep the ashes. Instead, at the cemetery, there is a grassy area just for spreading them. In the viewing room, I said hello to friends and family who came to pay their respect. I saw people that I had not seen in over thirty years and some of them I did not recognize (rough life in Belgium.) Benedicte begged me to come and look at dad, to see what a good job the mortician had done. Are you kidding me? No thanks, I can see his feet from here and that is enough. I believe that his soul is already gone so what you see is just the leftover envelope. My family is not that spiritual.

I was sitting next to my first cousin, Marilyn, and each time somebody came to shake my hand I would have to ask her, "who's this, who is that?"

They all said, "Oh you look just like your mom." or, "Oh you look just like your dad."

Make up your mind people.

We then drove to the cemetery for the cremation. Nadine was waiting for me there and right after the ashes were scattered, we got in her car to make our way over to my brother's house. She turned on the radio. The first song they were playing was my dad's favorite song. "Oh Carol," written in 1958 by Neil Sedaka.

My parents were fantastic dancers and used to dance to that song all the time. I thought *"Papa can you see me? Papa can you hear me?* Just kidding! This was too bizarre for words. Even Nadine knew about that song. We just looked at each other with open mouths. Was this a sign? Was he trying to tell me something? I always knew deep inside that my dad was proud of me even if he never told me. Family life could have been so good, but the poor man did not know any better. I forgive you dad, I won't forget, but I forgive you. I left for Miami the day afterwards.

Time flew by and a year later, right after Christmas, the concierge in our building asked Bob if he knew someone that wanted a Chihuahua puppy. The owner wanted to sell her. She was three months old.

Bob called me in Beverly Hills, "Let's just take her for one night to see how it goes."

Sure, one night!

Then we found out the story behind the puppy. One of the residents of the building, who happened to look and dress exactly like the actress Adrienne Barbeau, bought the dog for her daughter for Christmas and decided after a couple of days that the dog was too much to handle. She had kept the poor puppy locked in the shower 24 hours a day and never took her out for a walk. Of course, we kept that poor puppy. We named her Stella in honor of my father's fondness of the beer, Stella Artois.

When the ex-owner saw us walking Stella, she was like, "Oh, I didn't think you could take Chihuahuas out for walks. I thought they only like to be carried."

Are *you kidding me?* Months later, when she saw how good Stella was doing, she asked to buy her back. Can you believe the nerve of that woman? Up to this day, when Stella is misbehaving, we pick up the phone and tell Stella that we are calling Adrienne Barbeau to come and pick her up and Stella goes to hide!

Living in Miami, I can honestly say that there was never a dull moment. We made our way to parties, art galas, lavish hotels, condominiums openings, and private celebrity parties on Star Island. You name it, we went with our two best friends, Gigi and her husband Cisco. Gigi owned a spa called Touch on Miami Beach and was very well connected. It seemed like she got us every invitation. Moreover, if she could not snag an invite for us, we truly never needed one because she was the queen of talking her way into private parties.

At that time, I also began to do interior design. Clients were always asking for decorating advice and one day, Tamah, asked me to come over and give her a consultation and a proposal. Her place was in a high-rise on Key Biscayne. I went to work by editing and rearranging all the furniture, adding a new kitchen, and transforming one of the closets into an office. Bob did all the painting. When her friend Nicky, who lived a few floors below, saw the result, she hired me on the spot. Nicky gave me her credit card and said, "I will be gone for 4 months, I want a beach feeling to the place, don't call me until everything is finished and don't ask me for my opinion." Talk about an interior designer's dream.

I tore down walls and opened the whole place up. I created the feeling and look of living in the Greek islands. Four months later when, Nicky came back to Miami, she was beyond words. She loved it. My next customer, Steven, was a very wealthy bachelor who lived on Miami Beach and owned a townhouse in Washington DC. He was a total drug addict. I would have new furniture delivered and a week later, he would have already ruined it with booze and drugs. There was literally white powder everywhere. His boyfriend had two Yorkies and those poor dogs used to go around and smell the coke that was lying everywhere. They were constantly hyperactive; it broke my heart.

Steven did not care about anything in his place. I got him a $20,000 Robert Polidori photograph and he wanted it on the wall where the AC was running. Of course, with the Miami heat, it overran, and the frame was soaking wet.

The fun part for me during that time was going to the design showrooms. I loved that job. Anywhere I go I am always rearranging things. I think my dream job would be an accessories buyer.

CHAPTER ELEVEN

Peggy's Secrets

As usual, every five weeks I was back in Beverly Hills to work on my clients. Since my old salon was now closed, I rented a booth at Gavert Atelier, right on Brighton Way, across from Neiman Marcus and half a block from my old shop. I knew the owners, Stuart and his partner, Cody, since the mid 80's. When I would come into town, I also did Peggy's hair at her house in Beverly Hills. I started to notice that her health was worsening. On one visit, after her hair was done, I sat down in the kitchen to have dinner with her and her husband, Dr. H. She was joking around but something was not right. She looked somewhat disoriented. Then she asked Dr. H which pill she should take. He showed it to her and then fifteen minutes later, she looked even more out of it. She began slurring her words. It was very uncomfortable. She barely touched her food. Dr. H was going to drive me back to the hotel, just a few blocks away, and Peggy said she wanted to come, but she was very wobbly and could not decide on which coat to wear. He was losing his patience with her.

"What the fuck are you doing? Make up your mind and hurry up."

I had never seen the two of them like that before. They both dropped me off at the hotel. A week later, back in Miami, I got a phone call from her.

"Hi honey, it's Peggy. I just wanted to let you know before you hear it from someone else, I just left my husband."

"What?" I said. "What happened? What's going on? Are you okay? Are you in a safe place?"

"I'm ok now, I can't tell you on the phone, I'm in the Malibu house."

"Look, I said, we're meeting in Philadelphia very soon, right?"

"Of course, we have the television shopping network to work on. I can catch you up more then."

"Okay, take care of yourself."

And I hung up—concerned and in shock. I wondered if what happened in the house while I was there had anything to do with it.

A week later, I flew to Philadelphia where her chauffeur was waiting for me.

When I arrived at the hotel, I was back in the room that was adjacent to hers; there was a note under the door. It read, "Let me know when you arrive." I knocked on the door and she answered right away.

"Oh sweetie, I'm so glad to see you."

"So, what happened?"

I sat down next to her and she began to fill me in.

"Well, I woke up one day, and I got scared that Dr. H was going to hurt me."

"Are you serious?"

"Yes, even kill me maybe. So, I just took a book and my dog, Mayling, and left the house for good."

"And that's it?"

"Yes, I just left everything behind and moved into the Malibu house."

"Wow, I'm so sorry. I had no idea."

She nodded her head. "No one does, but the truth is we have been having problems for years. I tried to leave him once before. He begged me to come back, so I did. We even began seeing a marriage counselor."

She was silent a moment and I held her hand.

"So, did he hurt you?" She nodded.

"Yes, I have pictures of my arms and face with all the bruises. I kept them in a safe all this time."

She showed me the pictures.

"Oh my God, Peggy, did you call the police?"

"Yes, but in the end, I just didn't want to press charges. He promised me he was going to work on getting better."

"How did you stay? I mean why did you . . ."

"Well we haven't slept together for a long while. Truth is I can barely stand it when he touches me. He is terrible in bed. He's got no clue how to be sensual or to make love."

"I'm so sorry," I said.

"Oh, and then I discovered porn videos and pictures with transgender and transsexual content. I asked him why he had them and he said he was doing some research because he had been asked to perform a sex change on someone."

"Did you believe him?"

"No. Then I found out that he was having an affair with a famous interior designer. What an ass. I mean, I saved him twice from bankruptcy. I am done. I am filing for divorce this time. The guy is dangerous. I never thought about how dangerous until I realized that I never wanted him to do surgery on me in case he—"

"In case he what?"

"In case he . . . deliberately killed me."

"That's awful."

"Thank God I never needed surgery in that department! The only time I went under is when I left my TV series and I saw a plastic surgeon who did my eyes because I'd had just too many years of messy schedules, Quaaludes, cocaine and no sleep.

"Once," she added, "in a club with a girlfriend we snorted some coke in a stall and the vial rolled down underneath the door and there were people waiting in line to get into the stall. We didn't know what to do. We realized that if we both walked out, people would think that I was having sex with a woman in the toilet or, if they saw the vial rolling out, that I was a drug addict, or perhaps a 'drug addict lesbian.'"

We stayed up for hours and she told me everything that had been going on with her. She told me all about her beautiful house in Malibu. She wanted me to go back with her on a private plane and spend a few days with her and I thought it was a good idea. A couple of days later, we both were on that plane going to California.

Malibu Road

She was right. The house was gorgeous. It was on Malibu Road, north of Malibu colony. It was on the beach and, like all the houses on the beach, you only had a few feet of space on both sides to separate you from your neighbors. It was a very well-designed Hamptons-like beach house. From the street, all you saw was the garage. The entrance was on the left, and it took you down to a walkway. On your right was the guest's quarters, which contained two bedrooms and a bathroom. One of them was used as an ironing and laundry room. The other was a security office with TVs and cameras and a guard watching the propriety 24 hours a day. She truly feared for her life. She had been terrorized by her husband and by the paparazzi and to make matters worse, a stalker once left a dead deer in front of her garage for Thanksgiving and a dead bird on the kitchen door with blood all over it— even with all that security.

The main house consisted of a very nice foyer with a staircase on the right. On the left, the living, dining and sitting room over-looked the ocean. There was an Andy Warhol painting of Grace Kelly over the mantel. Down the hallway were two bedrooms and two bathrooms. One of them had been turned into an office and the other one would soon be my room. The house was less formal than the one in Beverly Hills. I found it very relaxing and serene with everything painted in soothing colors and lined with beautiful woodwork.

The kitchen was done in an all-white theme with Carrara marble. Up the stairs, on the right, a large master bedroom overlooked the ocean. A big mirror covered an entire wall and was facing the ocean, but behind that mirror was the shower. You could look at the water while showering but no one could look in. The master bathroom was not very big. From there you went to a big walk-in closet filled with hundreds of clothes. On the other side of the staircase, two more guest bedrooms and bathroom. One of them had stairs going up to a loft that she used as an exercise room and a place to meet with her therapist. The other bedroom was now a walk-in closet.

Her main housekeeper, Lorna, cooked and helped with the cleaning. Every drawer had a photo of what the tables and beds were supposed to look like so that everything could be put back in precise order. (LOVE IT!) The only thing I remembered from the previous house was a Picasso portrait above her bed, a small Rodin sculpture of a woman on the living room mantel and her dog, Mayling.

During my next visit, Peggy found out that Dr. H was going to take her to the cleaners. She had a pre-nup that would pay him one million dollars in the event of a divorce. Yet there was a credible rumor going around that she was going to give him eighty million dollars. She would not tell me exactly how much, but she said it was a lot. It is possible she just wanted him to keep quiet, chances are he had some dirt on her. Things got so bad that she took out a restraining order against him.

"Do you know that at the Beverly Hills house he started to spy on me by drilling a small hole in the wall between our two bathrooms so that he could hear all my conversations?"

I shook my head no.

"And all the jewelry that I told people he bought me over the years, I paid for all of it. Oh, and get this, every two years, he demanded a new Bentley. The truth is, I paid for everything he owns. He became so full of himself that he wanted to move to a huge estate in Mandeville Canyon."

I remember them showing me the floor plans. Peggy would say and do whatever she had to, to try to make him happy, hoping that he would somehow change, but that big estate was not her style at all.

"Now that I'm here in Malibu, why don't you stay here each time you come back to Beverly Hills after you are done with your clients? I will send a driver to pick you up, you could use the rest and I could use the company. We understand each other so well."

Once, at the Beverly Hills salon, she booked the last appointment of the day, so I could do her hair and afterwards go for dinner at Mr. Chow on Camden. I got the feeling that she wanted to be back in the news. *Fine with me. I am game.*

After I finished her hair, she touched up her makeup and her driver took us to the restaurant, which was only a block away. We had a wonderful dinner and when we left the paparazzi were waiting outside the restaurant to take some shots along with a few fans holding pictures for her autograph. I figured that she had called her publicist, so that he could alert the press that she was there with me, because, not only did they take pictures of me, they asked me questions. I said, "no comment." I made my way inside the limo while she posed for photos. The day after I was watching TV and on Entertainment Tonight, there we were, on screen, outside the restaurant with the headline, "Who's the new man in Peggy's life? Stay tuned tomorrow."

Apparently, I really disappointed some people when, the day after, the show announced that the man in Peggy Scott's life was her longtime friend and hairstylist, Jeremy Mariage. Well done, Peggy!

"Well, I'm so proud of you," she said. "You handled the paparazzi very well. You didn't say a word."

We continued to do photo shoots for the catalogue covers, usually an all-day affair flying me from Miami to Los Angeles, where a driver would pick me up at the airport, then take me to the hotel room. I have to say, thank God, I had her. I made a great income with all the work she gave me. She did not let anyone else do her hair. In a way, I sort of felt sorry for her. I started to feel that she was losing touch with reality. She became more and more of a recluse. As the months went on, she rarely left Malibu. I told her that she should get a small condominium in Beverly Hills or that area, just in case she wanted to spend a few days in town and see some friends. She often complained that no one wanted to drive out to Malibu to visit.

September 1, 2008

Bob and I went to Mexico City for my birthday. We were walking the street in Polanco when my phone rang.

"Hi honey, it's Peggy. Happy Birthday! I love you. I miss you. I just want you to know that you and I, we are a family and I think we need to be close together, so we can support each other."

I was not sure what to say but she continued.

"I have an offer that I don't think you guys can resist. I want you to move to Malibu. I am creating a house managing position for Bob starting at $30K a year plus health insurance and a car. And you can be my personal assistant for $65K a year."

"Wow, that's generous but— "

She continued, "I will take care of all the moving expenses, and for first, last and one month's deposit on a condo."

I was taken aback; I did not know what to say.

"Can you move now?" she asked.

I stayed on the phone with her for almost an hour and she continued with the, "I love you both, you are my family . . ."

"Listen, I said, that sounds amazing. However, my battery is almost dead, and we need to think about it. Give us a little time."

She gave us no time. She called every day and night, at random and intrusive times. I finally told her that we are in bed after 10:30 pm and that she should not call after that. I noticed that she sounded good in the morning, slower in the afternoon and loaded in the evening. *Was she tired or on something?*

I decided that I did not want to move. Bob, on the other hand, thought it was a great idea. It was an opportunity for him to have a new career and health insurance. I felt that I did not want to be with her every day. I knew that we would be expected to be a part of her life 24/7. On the top of that, I did not want to live in Malibu. Not only it was it too far to drive to Los Angeles due to the traffic, but also Malibu seemed extremely boring to me. I am a city person; I need some excitement, some lights and some action. That is why I was living in Miami. I was not ready to retire in Malibu, but she would not let up. She promised me lots of time off. *Well, thank you very much!* Then she began emailing us every day.

If I did not answer back right away, she would call every phone. "Where are you? You avoiding me? I miss you. I love you."

I felt like she was almost becoming obsessed with me. She sent Bob a book for him to learn the business of estate management. I knew that she had nobody in her life besides her staff. During one conversation, she told me that her mother, who lived in Atlanta, had emphysema and lupus and was dying.

"I'm paying for 24-hour nursing care, and my sister lives next door to her. I'm sure that she just wants to make sure when mother dies, that it would be easier for her to get a hold of mother's cash."

Peggy said that she had been paying her sister and husband's bills for years.

"I'm furious, on the top of that, mother had just sold a story about me to the tabloids."

I thought, for a dying woman that seemed like a lot of strength.

"Mother abused me since I was a child. She used to beat me and lock me up in the closet for hours and tell me that I was "good for nothing.""

Yet, at the same time, she pushed Peggy to be a star. She hated Peggy because she looked just like her father, who by the way, she said, knew about the abuse, but looked the other way.

After that, it started to get somewhat creepy. She knew my schedule when I was in Beverly Hills and of course, she wanted me to come and stay with her for an extra day or two. I felt I just could not refuse her, so I went. I was usually very tired from working all day. I would tell myself, *can't believe I have to go there and entertain her for a few days . . .* But spending all that time with her started to make me ill. I felt that when I was with her I had to be "on" all the time. If I would get quiet for a moment she was like, "Is something wrong? It is, isn't it? I know it, I can feel it."

Strange behavior

Barely back in Miami, she called.

"Hi honey, it's Peggy. I need help with my closet and I know how much you love to organize things. I asked my stylist how much she would charge to do it. She said $2,500 per day. I think I will need four days. What if you take the job instead?"

$10K for four days of work. Wow, that is a great offer. She really wanted me to be with her in Malibu. The next week I flew back to the west coast. The driver picked me up at the airport and we took the long drive to Malibu. After being dropped off, I settled in my bedroom. Then I visited with Lorna, the housekeeper. We tried to be quiet because if Peggy heard us from upstairs, she would think that Lorna was not working.

"She sometimes does the oddest thing." She started. "In the morning she will request a big dinner like a whole turkey, veggies, rice, soup and salad. Then, in the evening when it is about time to eat, she decides she is just going to have oatmeal instead. Everything I cooked just sits in the fridge. The day after, she says she's no longer in the mood for it and tells me to throw it all away."

Lorna was not lying. I witnessed the routine myself after that. I asked Peggy why she did not give it to the staff. Her answer was, "I pay them very well. They can afford their own food."

Her personal assistant worked from the home office. Peggy also had another business office, Peggy Scott Productions on Pacific Coast Highway, a ten-minute ride from her house, where other employees worked. At exactly 9 am every day, she would call to see if someone answered the phone. If they would answer the phone one minute late, she would remind them of that.

"Do you know I have been calling since 9:00 am and its 9:01? Where is everyone?"

At 5 pm, one of them would have to drive to the house to give her the report of the day along with all the paperwork.

It was always in an envelope. In big letters would be written, "FOR HER EYES ONLY."

On that first evening at the house, she wanted to try on some clothes. She was going to a Bar Mitzvah the next weekend. She was talking very mellow. I was almost positive that she had taken something. I was complaining about my back hurting from the plane ride and she said she had some Demerol pills left over from a long time ago. She handed me a silver pillbox with five inside. She was not sure if they were still good. I was afraid to take one in case, with my luck with medicine, I was to have a reaction. She went back to trying on some clothes. She had an insane amount of clothing on rolling racks. It looked like a department store. A lot of them still had their tags. There were purses with prices hanging off them for thousands of dollars. Endless piles of shoes, scarves and costume jewelry everywhere.

"Peggy, aren't you afraid to leave all this merchandise lying around."

"No honey, I don't care, you know I have a gun."

Soon, I was thinking about taking a pill because my back was just hurting too much. I opened the pillbox and two were missing. "What happened to the two Demerol?"

"Oh, I thought I'd try them to see if they were still good."

She began to talk nonsense. It was getting later and later but she would not stop. If I did not give her full attention, she was back on, "What's wrong? Are you ok?"

No wonder nobody wants to stay with her.

"Peggy, its past midnight and I need to go to bed because my body is still on Miami time."

"Okay Honey. You should get to bed. Can I come in for some cuddling?"

I looked at her oddly.

"You know it's nothing sexual."

"Peggy, I'm exhausted. I just need to get some sleep."

Less than an hour later, I wake up to hear a scratching noise behind the door.

"Jeremy, are you sleeping? Can I come in?"

Silence.

"Jeremy? Jeremy?"

I faked snoring and she stopped. I wanted to cry. I was so tired. At one point, I wanted to pinch myself to see if this was really a nightmare. The next day at breakfast, she tells me that I cannot be her personal assistant because the job is too demanding, and I am no good with computers.

"But, I have a great idea," she says.

"Oh yeah, what's that?"

"You should be a social worker and find an older woman in Beverly Hills to be a companion to. You could take her to all her appointments, take her shopping and do her hair so that she would look good all the time."

She said I should take a CPR class (which I ended up taking later figuring it would always be good information to know.) The next day she changed her mind.

"I want you to take care of me when I'm older or ill. We could be together 24 hours. You can do my hair and make-up and dress me too. You know, I just have this feeling that I will die when I'm 64."

Later, that afternoon she told me that she just signed a contract with Richard Branson of Virgin Airlines for $250,000 to fly into space.

"Oh, and did you know that I am the only woman on the list and I've been training with a specialist."

Then she admitted to me that she was having an affair with a married man with two kids. She showed me his picture. He was very good looking with dark hair.

"It had been going on for a while, but I don't think he's ready to leave his wife and I don't want to destroy his marriage because of the kids. Oh, and I am still seeing Mick— a camera operator and a very nice guy, client of mine. Although I don't know where it can lead," she said, "because physically he reminds me of my father, especially when we have sex!"

I noticed more strange behavior. In the evening when the phone would ring, she would pick it up and disguise her voice telling the person on the line that either, Peggy was not home or that they had reached a wrong number. Wouldn't be easier not to answer the phone, I asked myself. One afternoon she decided to go spy on her office staff at the Pacific Coast Highway office. We drove over there, parked and then we had to walk completely against the walls because "there are cameras." We made our way up to the office. There were large windows. We could not walk in front of them because "they would see us" so we both began crawling on our hands and knees trying to reach the front door unnoticed. Of course, the staff was there working. They knew better. They should have hired her for "Mission Impossible."

Back at the house, she wanted to go to the newsstand down the street.

"I have a plan," she said. "You should wear sunglasses and a hat, take the SUV and drive the opposite direction of the newsstand so that the paparazzi would follow you, thinking you're me. Meanwhile, I will take the Mercedes to the stand."

I told her no.

She replied, "Fine, plan number two. I do not want them seeing me buying gossip magazines. How about if you drive the SUV and park in front of the newsstand."

Deal I said. We both got in the car.

"Here's some cash for you to buy Star, US, Globe and The Enquirer."

We drove down. (It is a five-minute walk by the way.) I was on the left side of the stand buying the gossip rags and she was on the right-side buying fashion magazines. Then we met to pay. I paid for mine, and she paid for hers and we both got back in the car.

Damn, we really fooled those paparazzi!

It was actually very funny. Why would they chase Peggy while Paris Hilton and Britney Spears were renting houses a couple blocks away? In a way, I felt sad for her and many other celebrities who somewhere inside knew that their time was over—that nobody wanted to take their pictures anymore.

The funniest thing of all of that was that when I was in the car I had a problem with the brakes, so she looked down at them but kept moving her body and head up and down in my crotch area. We laughed because it looked like she was giving me a blowjob. Now, *that* would have been a great picture (and would make the headlines.)

Later, she said she wanted to move to a different neighborhood. That the beach in front of her house is now a public beach and she felt that too many people were walking by.

She continued, "Also I know that the water is rising because a couple of years ago, the patio used to have seven steps going down to the sand and now they have four."

We went to check it out and you could see that the steps were disappearing in the sand.

"You know, I got an all cash offer for $24,000,000 from designer James Perse."

"Are you going to take it? Your first offer is always your best one."

"I really don't know, he wants to install dark hardwood floors."

"Who cares what he does, you are getting $24,000,000." I said.

"Maybe I should move a little further north, to Point Dume or build an estate in Brentwood."

"What a fantastic idea," I answered.

"Well, you know if I do that, I could build a guest house, so you and Bob could live close to me."

She had a real estate friend who was looking around for possibilities. That afternoon, at the house, we had a meeting with her psychologist. Peggy told him all the plans she had for us. She also told him that if someday something "happened to Bob," then I would move in with her full time.

"Jeremy, you are now in my will, so you don't have to worry for the rest of your life, I will take care of you."

The doctor seemed to approve everything she said.

That evening, while lounging on the sofa, she remembered a very funny story that happened with her and Bette Davis. It was years before, when she was just starting out as an actress. She was at La Costa spa near San Diego and was about to get a massage. The therapist said that her next client was Bette Davis and Peggy said that she really wanted to meet her. After the massage was over, the therapist left the room, leaving Peggy with a small towel that was big enough to cover either the top or the bottom of her body. She decided on the bottom. As she left the room and started walking down the hallway, along comes Bette, who happened to be stark naked smoking a cigarette. The therapist said to her, "Miss Davis, this is Peggy Scott, a young actress who's dying to meet you." Bette looks Peggy up and down and says, "Quite big tits you have," then she puffed smoke in her face and just kept walking.

So Bette!

Then Peggy went on about Randy Gibson, from the Gibson brothers' famous group and how much she had tried to steer him in the right direction.

"I loved him so much, and I tried to help him so many times, but he wouldn't listen at all. Did you know that we recorded a song together?"

"What, are you kidding? Do you have it?'

"Of course, let's go upstairs, I'll play it for you."

It was a ballad, not too bad. Their love affair ended when she gave him a choice.

"I told him, 'Randy you going to have to choose now, it's me or it's your drugs.'"

Of course, he chose the drugs.

Later that evening, we were watching *Lois and Bertrand*, a movie about Lois Luke and Bertrand Rafferty. Lois was one of the richest women in the world, and the last few years of her life, Bertrand was her butler and companion. Lois became very sick and she only allowed Bertrand to see her. When she died, she left him her fortune, and rumors started that he killed Lois by giving her a heavy dose of drugs.

When the movie ended, Peggy looked at me and said, "You know, they loved each other; the last thing on his mind was to kill her. We were friends with him. Dr. H was friends with Lois' doctors and nurses. The doctors were planning to eliminate her so they could be on the board of her estate and remove Bertrand out of the picture. They promised Dr. H he could be on the board if he helped them with their plans. They said I would get some of Lois' jewelry if I would go along with it. However, I declined. I told him I didn't want to be involved."

She went on to say that Dr. H had already been planning trips to New York to be on the board of directors for Lois' trust. And that when it was time for her to die, he would deliver all the morphine necessary to make Lois go away. What nobody knew is that Lois left control of everything to Bertrand. A couple of years later when he died, with no heirs, he left everything to Lois' foundation. The story was all over the newspapers.

This was heavy stuff. If her story was true, she could have gone to the police and had Dr. H arrested. Or, she could have made a deal with him on the divorce and saved herself a lot of money. . . It's hard to imagine. Dr. H was too smart to get involved in that kind of situation. He could have lost his practice and tarnished his reputation, not to mention gone to jail!

I really started to wonder if she was making up that story to discriminate against Dr. H. or if she was getting delusional herself!

Peggy looked at me and said, "We can be like them, me Lois, and you Bertrand!"

After that, we watched the late news and went to bed. Lying in bed, I remembered one day, from a couple of years back at her Beverly Hills house, we had been chitchatting in her bedroom when Dr. H stopped by to say he was leaving.

"Are you going to work?" Peggy asked.

"No," he answered. "I'm going to play golf."

She then looked at me and said, "Well, at least nobody will to die today."

I just could not believe she said that.

During my visit, I asked her many times, "Peggy, when are we starting your closet? I have a great plan to organize everything."

"Not now Honey, later, later."

I began to realize that she did not intend to do her closet at all, that I was just there to keep her company. Fine with me. She had recorded the TV series *The Tudors*. We tried to watch three episodes a day. One evening she wanted to go see a movie in the Malibu theatre.

They were playing *Burn after Reading* with Brad Pitt and George Clooney. It was a small theatre just two minutes from the house. I was fine with it but of course leaving the house was this huge production.

"We have to try to avoid the paparazzi!"

(*Not again!*)

She got all dressed in black, black sunglasses and a black hat. In addition, she wanted me to do the same. She told me she had a plan. (*No more plans, please.*)

I should take the Porsche and drive first so the paparazzi will think it is she and then she will follow me to the theatre. She will leave five minutes later with the Mercedes and she will park at the opposite end of the parking lot. Fine as long as I do not have to dress up. The whole production was a movie in and of itself. (*By the way, nobody followed us.*) We were the first ones there. I bought two tickets and went inside. We sat in the last row, which only had two seats. Inside, she kept on her sunglasses on so not to be recognized.

Then Brian Grazer, a big movie producer, walked into the theater and sat down. She spotted him and bending over, she went across the room to speak to him.

When she got back she said, "I just had to apologize to him because I saw him on the beach not long ago and I thought that he might be interested in me because he was divorcing his wife. I just wanted to tell him that I was not interested."

Then she leans in to tell me that the only real contender for her affections now was Richard Branson from Virgin, but unfortunately, he's married so that probably wouldn't work. This continued during the previews. Every time she saw somebody she knew, she ran over on all fours to say hello, then removed her sunglasses only for them.

Why don't they have wine in this theater? I could use some right now.

When the movie was over, we both got into our cars and drove home to watch the *Tudors*. I got ice cream and she had a beer.

She said that the cosmetic company, which produced Cindy Crawford's line of cosmetics wanted to cancel her because she did not sell enough. Peggy thought that Cindy was not approachable nor a good sales person either. I began to wonder why it had been so long since we had been back Philadelphia. I wondered if there might be a problem with Peggy and her own company. I did not want to ask any questions in case I would upset her.

The day after she said, "I hate your sunglasses; let's go shopping for your birthday."

We went shopping for a late birthday gift at Malibu Country Mart, a big outdoor mall where all the celebs hang when they are in Malibu. At the eyeglasses store, she wanted me to try on a pair of "Chrome Hearts." This went on and on for thirty minutes. I admit, I am very difficult with sunglasses. She liked one in particular. I did not, and they were $1500.

She kept saying, "Take them, take them."

All I was thinking was, *that is three payments on my car.*

I finally found a pair that was okay. They were $800 and even that was so expensive. She kept insisting.

"Jeremy, I won't leave the shop until we buy them, I can buy anything I want, so the price is no problem."

After that, we went across the street to James Perse. She made me try on some cotton sweaters. She wanted me to get three at $200 each. We then went around the corner to pick up an order of fish and salads at an Italian restaurant. That bill was close to $250 for the two of us.

The next day I flew back home to Miami. I told her that I would be back in two weeks to go look for a place to live. I was suddenly forcing myself, making plans to live there. I started doing research for some potential rentals online. I thought the perfect compromise would be to live somewhere between Malibu and Beverly Hills, maybe Santa Monica or Pacific Palisades. I made an appointment with a real estate agent. When I got back to Los Angeles, Peggy wanted to come with me to look at what he might have found. We saw a nice condo in Pacific Palisades, off Sunset Boulevard. The agent was showing us the place and Peggy embarrassed me.

She acted as if I was not there at all, telling the agent, "Well, this is not going to work, and this room is not bright enough and the noise from Sunset is too loud and Jeremy needs a pool."

A pool? I do not even swim.

The other option was a loft in Santa Monica and I thought it was perfect. However, for her, that would not do either.

Back at the house, she got upset. "Look, this is not the deal we made. I wanted you to be near me. Santa Monica is just too far away."

"But I's only thirty minutes to your house," I said.

"But what if something happens to me? It would take you too long to get here. Also, it's not fair to Bob who has to drive every day to work in all that traffic."

"Look, I just can't afford Malibu. I can spend a maximum of $2,500 on a monthly rent."

She was now adamant.

"This is important to me, whatever you find in Malibu, I will cover the difference. We can sign a six-month lease with an option to renew for another six. I am sure that in six months I will buy a much bigger property for all of us. You know, so we can all live together."

She called her agent who took me to see some possibilities.

It was a very nice complex, like a resort, but it was fifteen minutes further north of her and in the middle of nowhere, close to Zuma Beach. They had a concierge, gym, pool, and a car service that would take you anywhere you want. She pressured me heavily. She started major negotiations with the leasing agent of the complex. They were asking $6,500 a month in rent, although Peggy got them down to $4,000. She said that she would pay the difference of $1,500 each month so I could be fifteen minutes away and this was just temporary anyway since very soon we were all going to live on the same property.

I signed the lease, but I knew deep down, that by being so close, she would be calling me all the time to come over. (God I was right.)

After signing the lease, I drove back to her house and now, she was happy. As we sat down in the living room, she said, "I have been participating in stem cell treatments for my illness and I'm flying on a regular basis to the Dominican Republic; it's completely legal there. In addition, on some occasions, I fly to Mexico for treatment. You know, this all had to be done in secret because kidnapers might abduct me if they found out I was there. The last time I was there, I took a private plane to Mexico where I hired a driver along with several bodyguards. Well, someone must have let the cat out of the bag because when I arrived in Mexico, a car began following us. I saw that the men in the other car were carrying guns. They got up close to my car and tried to ram it. However, thanks to my driver's skills, he was able to lose them, and I was taken to my destination to have the treatment done. Fortunately, no one was waiting for me when I made my way back to the airport."

The following day, I flew back to Miami. As soon I got back, Bob, at Peggy's request, was on the phone with one of her employees regarding the moving expenses. He interviewed three companies and we went for the middle price. Peggy wired $6,447.00 right away. The next time I would see her would be when we moved there. One more time, we said goodbye to friends.

December, 2008

A few days before Christmas, we left Florida for our drive to Dallas to spend Christmas with Carol, Bob's mother. Snow blanketed the landscape. We saw friends who used to work at my salon and had dinner with them. We finally reached Malibu by New Year's. Bob's lease was up on his car, so we only had mine. What we did not know was that Peggy had a hidden agenda. As a Christmas present, she rented us a hotel room at the Marriot in Westlake Village until our furniture arrived in Malibu.

For New Year's Eve's dinner, she had planned for us to go to Nobu, the famous sushi restaurant in Malibu. Funny because she knows I do not eat sushi. She said that she had worked with the chef to create a special menu for her and her guests. Those guests included her former assistant, Lauren and her husband, then Bob and me. She also invited her publicist, but he canceled on her at the last minute. She seemed upset about his cancelation. Bob and I went to her home an hour early, so I could do her hair. Lauren and her husband arrived exactly on time at 6:45 pm. Peggy had not planned anything for her guests, so I told her to open a bottle of champagne and get some nuts to nibble. She said there was no time because we must leave by 6:55 and alcohol was not a good idea because Lauren's husband was a recovering alcoholic.

So why do the rest of us have to suffer?

I told her that I was sure it wasn't the first time he had had to be around people who were drinking, plus, it's New Year's Eve! Chances are he would be seeing some drinking that night. The whole experience was very awkward. We all stood there in front of the kitchen counter starring at each other. Then it was time to leave for Nobu. Peggy, Bob, a bodyguard, the chauffeur and myself in one car while the others followed behind. When we got there, the place was empty. Of course, nobody but us would celebrate New Year's Eve at 7 pm.

After being seated, we all looked at the menu as Peggy explained to us the weeks of preparation she and the chef had done to plan this wonderful dinner. Nobody was drinking so, of course, I ordered a Cosmopolitan. On my way to the bathroom, I looked at an empty table and saw that their menu was the same menu as ours.

Why would she tell us that she designed the menu? Nobody needs the drama. I do not understand what she had to prove, unless she's starting to completely lose it? That wouldn't surprise me after the stories she's been telling lately!!

I did not touch my plate since I do not eat raw food; I was on a liquid diet that evening!

The next day, sitting in the living room having tea, she explained to both of us why she now had a bodyguard.

"The day after Christmas, I almost shot Isabel."

"The new housekeeper? Why?" Bob asked.

"Well, Mayling, my dog, needs to be walked at the same time every day for twenty minutes. She walks her ten minutes up the coast to the end of the block and ten minutes back. Well, Isabel was taking about 45 minutes."

"So?

"So, she was planning on kidnapping the dog!"

Bob and I exchanged looks.

She continued, "Then, she finally came back from the walk and she entered the foyer carrying the dog. She did not put it down because her paws needed cleaning first. Well, I was waiting for her at the top of the stairs with a gun, and I told her "put the dog on the floor."

Bob and I looked at each other wondering what the hell kind of situation we had moved ourselves into.

"So, did she put the dog on the floor?" Bob asked.

Peggy replied, "She was acting all strange and I really couldn't tell what she was going to do, and she moved toward me like, sort of, well I felt threated. She was going to do something to the dog. Then the other housekeeper walked in and I told her to get away from Isabel so that she would not get blood and brains splattered on her because I was going to shoot her in the head. Isabel just totally freaked out and ran to the back of the house and locked herself in with the dog and then she called 911."

"What did you do?" I asked.

"Well, I waited outside of the doorway and when the police arrived, I told them how she had become a threat. Therefore, they escorted her out, but no charges were filed. And get this, the next day she went to the police and filed a complaint against me for attempted murder and kidnapping!"

First, she shot her dog few years ago and now almost the housekeeper. Who is next? Peggy should be locked up and have that gun taken away from her!

Bob and I found out later that another housekeeper filed a complaint against her for extreme and unnecessary stress. She told the police she was losing sleep and could not work there anymore. I did not want to scare Bob, but I was starting to think that this situation with Peggy's lies and craziness was already just too much for us.

Peggy's birthday

A few days after the New Year, Peggy decided to venture all the way out to Beverly Hills for lunch at La Scala for her birthday. It was nothing short of a full production. Bob and I arrived at her house early so that I could do her hair. She was concerned about her outfit and feared that it was not age appropriate. She had just planned to wear jeans and a black leather jacket, but for a full fifteen minutes, she debated whether she should wear an "open or closed zipper" on the jacket.

She would zip it up and ask, "Does it look better in a photo-op like this?"

I gently guided her to choose a style and get in the car, so we would not be late for her friend that was meeting us at the restaurant. The minute we got in the SUV, she started complaining about the paparazzi following her.

"I'm so tired of having to deal with them, I really wish that I could drive my car by myself, but I just couldn't with them following me everywhere."

She did not stop; she went on and on. She was manically going over the same information when I almost turned around and yelled, "Shut up woman, are you on speed?" but Bob beat me to it by saying, "Peggy, I've been checking behind us and there is no one following us."

She answered by saying, "Well, it's the off season and the paparazzi are on vacation right now."

I laughed so hard. If there was one profession that never took a vacation, it is the paparazzi.

She kept quiet for the rest of the drive into Beverly Hills. We arrived at La Scala and she made her grand entrance.

We sat down, and she ordered their famous chopped salad but before she could take a bite, she began complaining of stomach issues. Then the conversation was all about how she got Robert Downey Jr. his role in the Iron Man movie.

"Because of his drug problem, no one wanted to hire him. However, I am coaching him and as a thank you, I am going to play his mother for the sequel. However, do not say anything to anyone. This is all hush hush."

I could not wait for him to say, "Hello Mother," in one of the scenes. After a long verbose lunch, she wanted to go shopping. Our first stop was at Cartier because she wanted a new watch. She told me she was going to give me her Cartier Pasha watch the minute she bought a new one. She made her way inside and told the salesperson that she wanted to view her selections in a private room. She spent about an hour looking, while Bob and I waited in the lobby. She did not buy anything. Our next stop was at another jewelry store. Then another. Same song and dance with no purchase luck whatsoever. Then the driver picked us up and drove us back to Malibu.

Lovely birthday.

Our furniture finally arrived from Miami and we left the hotel in Westlake to move to Point Dume.

The following week, Bob was at the grocery store in Zuma Beach waiting in line to pay. There was a woman in a t-shirt and bathrobe in front of him. He was barely paying attention, reading a magazine while he waited.

"I don't know, she said, I thought that card would work. Try this one."

The checkout person tried that card and shook his head "no."

The woman spent about five minutes handing over cards that were solemnly rejected, one by one.

"I don't get it. That one should have worked!"

The woman was getting louder and more upset by the moment. Bob felt badly for this tired, haggard sounding woman. Finally, he looked up to see who it was . . . Pamela Anderson. No makeup, t-shirt and bathrobe and no money to pay for groceries. Bob was so upset to see one of his favorite actresses, someone that he had said if he was straight, would be the first woman he would go to bed with. What a disappointment! After that, Angelina Jolie replaced Pamela. (That is okay, I went for Brad anyway.)

The house manager

Bob's new job was to be Peggy's house manager. He was supposed to oversee organizing and running everything concerning the maintenance and staff. He would also be driving her on errands around the local neighborhood. Right away, Peggy bought him a car in case he needed to drive her or pick things up for the house, etc. She wanted to make sure that the car would be good enough for her to be seen getting in and out of. Therefore, Bob got a black Ford Escape SUV. She had the windows tinted and installed a state-of-the-art navigation system. Funny thing about that car . . . each time we went somewhere she would always call Bob to see where he/we were going. This only happened when we drove Bob's car. Later on, when the car was sold, we found a tracking device underneath it. We could never prove who had put it there. James Bond Scott.!!

Bob was supposed to start on January 2, 2009. The first week Peggy was feeling too weak for him to start. The second week she had meetings, so she told us that she could not be at the house to provide him with instructions. Finally, on the third week, she sent Bob to her office for half the day and then instructed him to work the rest of the day at her house.

She said to him, "I want you to know the scoop on everything."

She gave him files compiled like a book to read on all the people that worked for her. There was a chapter about me that contained all my likes and dislikes, what seats I liked on planes, what kind of car I liked to be picked up in, what kind of hotel room I preferred, and instructions to make sure that her room would always be adjacent to mine. I felt honored that she cared so much.

After Bob's second day at work, she called us at 11:30 pm.

"Sweetie, its Peggy, I need for both of you to come to the house right now."

"Are you OK, what's the matter?" I asked.

"Can't tell you on the phone, it's very important, I need you right away."

"Are you sure?"

"Yes, it cannot wait until morning," she answered back.

Well, this better be good! We were already in bed and did not want to go anywhere, yet we wearily drove over to her house. When we got there, fifteen minutes later, we were escorted by the security to the front door.

"Oh, I'm so happy to see you both, I have fantastic news."

The three of us sat down and she started.

"You know Sheeba, the hairdresser who does my extensions? [Peggy had lost a lot hair from God knows what.] She is ready to work with you and introduce you to some of her clientele."

I stared at her, exhausted. *That is what couldn't wait until the next morning?*

"Isn't that fantastic news, you know she does all the celebrities in town, like Beyoncé."

Yeah, fantastic, it's midnight!

She continued, "And I want to let you know that Bob is doing such a wonderful job and that in no time he will go very far in the business and that pretty soon, I will give him a raise."

I sighed and tried to make it to the door.

"Okay, we are really tired, and my back is hurting so we are going home now."

She practically stood in front of us and said, "Wait, let me give you a massage so you will sleep much better tonight."

Bob rolled his eyes. She asked me to lay on the floor behind the sofa. She went on and on about how she was a "healer" who often went to the hospital to cure children and adults with incurable diseases. This was very hush hush, she said, as she did not want the public and the press to know about it.

"Really, it's true, just by touching them, they heal."

Wondered if she could turn water to champagne?

Hallelujah, hallelujah!

The following day she wanted Bob to work full time at the office. Lunch was always to be between noon and 1 pm, however on this day, Bob and the office assistant didn't get out until around 12:30 pm because the phones had just been too busy. Bob asked the assistant if they should be back by 1 pm anyway since Peggy expected lunch to be over at 1 pm. She told him no, but maybe he should go get lunch and bring it back to the office so that they could eat it there. Bob went to get lunch and returned at 1:05 pm. He did not have the keys and the assistant had not arrived back yet, so he waited outside the door. Peggy called Bob on his cell demanding to know why no one was in the office. Bob tried to explain what had happened, but she did not want to hear it. She ordered him to return to her house immediately. Bob ate his lunch on the way there. When he opened the front door, she hit him with a barrage of questions about where, when, and why he and the assistant were not in the office at 1 pm.

"And why are you chewing gum?"

Bob explained that he had taken a piece of gum after his bite of hamburger so that he did not offend her. She stuck her hand out and told him to spit it out. She then took the rest of his lunch and threw it away saying that "lunch" was over.

"I'm sure you are chewing gum because you've been drinking!" She added.

"No, it was because the burger had onions," he said.

"I want you to go right away to a center and be tested for alcohol consumption."

Bob got worried and all he could think about was that gun in the house.

Peggy called me as soon as possible to tell me the story.

"Well, you know I had the housekeeper search through his lunch bag to see what Bob had eaten and found that indeed, onions were on the burger and you know, there's two things that are never allowed in my house, gum and onions."

She sent him back to our house for the rest of the day.

The next day, she called Bob.

"I want you to bring back right away all the notes that you have taken so far. In addition, I have decided to pay you three months' salary for NOT working."

She fired him on the spot. Her plan was now in full swing. Bob was confused—wondering if she was completely nuts. He went to her house to drop off his notes.

Lorna, the housekeeper, told him to go into the garage because she wanted to know what had happened. Bianca, the other housekeeper was there too. They asked why Peggy had fired him.

"Well, Peggy said that the two housekeepers—you guys—had told her that you couldn't work with me. I wasn't sure what I had done because I'd only spent about half a day at the house."

They both shook their heads confused.

"Oh no, no, no, we never said anything like that. In fact, we said just the opposite; we were so thrilled to have you there to help out."

Bob dropped off his notes and left—completely perplexed.

I was working in Beverly Hills that day. On my way back to Malibu, Peggy called, and wanted to see me immediately. I stopped at her house and once there, she started.

"You know that Bob was completely drunk, and I had to fire him. What are you going to do when Bob goes away?"

I took a step back asking, "Away where?"

She replied, "Well I'm going to pay him for three months' salary, so he can leave town. I mean come on, with a new car and cash in his hand, he will leave."

"Excuse me?" I said.

"Yes, and then you can move in with me. Don't worry, you can bring all your dogs."

After getting over the initial shock, I told her that Bob was not going anywhere. Nevertheless, she would not let up.

"Jeremy, you don't realize how serious the situation is. You will not believe what he did. I cannot protect him anymore."

"What happened?"

"Well, all I can say is that the police and my lawyers are now involved. I just can't protect him anymore."

I kept asking her over and over what happened.

"Call Bob right now and tell him to come over for a meeting immediately."

I did, and he rushed over. I opened the door and asked him, "What did you do?"

However, before he could answer, she called Lorna and the security guard to join us at the dining room table.

Bob was stunned, "I can't believe that you're calling in security . . . for me?"

"Well I want them here, so I can have witnesses."

We all sat down, and she said, "Bob, I need an apology from you."

"An apology for what?" he asked.

"I want you to apologize to me because you made a mistake."

The security person rolled his eyes—you could tell he was thinking, *what the fuck*?

She kept on, repeating to Bob, "Admit it, you made a mistake."

Bob insisted that he had nothing to apologize for which only seemed to inflame her.

She turned to Bob with vehemence.

"You should be arrested for trespassing on my property. You were not invited to come inside the house when you were dropping off your notes."

"I never came inside the house," he answered. "And I was in the garage talking to the housekeepers, only after Lorna invited me."

Peggy turned to her. "Is that true?"

"Yes, I did, Miss Scott."

She was getting redder and redder by the minute— though she never lost her calm tone.

"Thank you, Lorna, you are dismissed for the day. Go home."

"Look Bob, because of your actions, I simply cannot protect you anymore. You are going to be named in the lawsuit."

She was referring to the lawsuit where her housekeeper was suing her over the gun incident.

She continued, "I want you to admit that you made a mistake coming into the house to talk to the housekeepers."

Then it came out. What she really wanted. She wanted Bob to testify against Isabel. (The gun stories.)

"Look, Peggy I can't be named in the lawsuit. I wasn't a witness to anything that occurred that day."

"But you know what happened. I told you what happened."

"Peggy, I only know one side of that story and that's yours."

This answer did not please her at all. She began a tirade that lasted for thirty minutes or so. That poor security guard, I felt so bad for him.

Occasionally I would just shake my head and say, "I can't believe we are really sitting here dealing with all this crap!"

She would respond, "You see what he did? That's why I cannot protect him anymore."

Finally, I had had enough. We stood up and said that we were leaving. She repeated one more time to Bob, "You need to apologize!"

Bob spat out, "Okay, I'm sorry you feel that I owe you an apology."

She was stunned. She then told the guard to escort Bob off her property and asked me to stay behind. I did not want to, but I thought maybe I could diffuse the tension.

Bob told me later that the security guard apologized to him for having to go through that and Bob told him that it was okay, "She's pretty crazy."

Meanwhile, back in the house, she kept on her rant.

"You've seen what Bob did, and it just makes sense to send him away and then you can move in here. I will sell the house and buy something different for the two of us."

Totally delusional—there was no breaking through. I told her that I was done talking and that I was going home.

God knows why I continued to do her hair a few more times. In addition, each time she would pressure me to leave Bob.

When I would not comply with her request, she said, "You know Jeremy, I have thought about this long and hard and I decided that I cannot work with you anymore unless and until you leave Bob and come live with me. I am no longer going to pay the supplement on your rent and that effective this moment I am cutting you off completely."

I told her that I was in California because of her and then she asked, "What have you ever done for me?"

Are you kidding me?

Cutting the cord

On February 28, I sent her an email asking about the rent. I told her that I could not afford $4000 per month, especially since Bob was no longer working. However, after twenty-four years, she simply dismissed me. I could not figure it or her out. *Why was she punishing me?*

She would just repeat, "Why should I help you if you are not helping me?"

A few days later, she called me. Her voice was flat, matter of fact.

"Jeremy, it's Peggy. I am calling you to let you know this will be the last time we will ever be speaking. I have turned your letter over to my lawyers and to the Los Angeles District Attorney and I'm planning on charging you with extortion."

She made it clear that the only way she would stop her proceedings is if I decided to leave Bob right way.

"Choose now. It's Bob or me."

I started to tell her that that would never happen, but she cut me off and said, "Listen! This is the last I'm telling you . . ."

I cut her OFF faster and said, "Now YOU shut up and YOU listen, for the last time EVER Peggy, I am not going to choose you over Bob. That's the way it is and the way it is always going to be, enough is enough!"

She hung up the phone. Ten minutes later, her attorney called.

"What's going on between you two?" he asked.

I sighed, knowing that he was trying to get information that they could use against me. I told him nothing, knowing for sure that she was listening on her phone line. The next day I got an email from her telling me that she will be reporting everything she had ever given us, including gifts, to the IRS.

And that was it.

All those years down the drain? Was she slowly going crazy all this time? Was everything she told me about Dr. H. a lie? Maybe he was the lucky one and escaped just in time before she went down loony?

I was now feeling so sorry for him. She could have caused him huge troubles for actions that she may have dreamed of! The guy deserved every dollar to have put up with that craziness all those years!!!

Bob and I realized that she had planned everything out. I said yes to everything she demanded or requested. I said yes because she promised Bob she would create a job for him, even sending him books to study on how to manage estates. She offered to pay for the move, help with our rent, pay extra expenses, open a salon for me in Malibu and do her hair four times a week at $150 per session. She wanted me to travel everywhere with her as a companion for business and pleasure. After six months, her plan was to buy a condominium for Bob and me or build a guesthouse on a new property that she wanted to buy in Malibu or Brentwood. All this was so that I could be close to her because now we were her only family. That was what she had told us.

However, the truth was that she never intended to hire Bob at all. It did not make sense the way she lavishly praised him telling him what a wonderful job he was doing and then suddenly firing him because of a hamburger. It was clear, she wanted me for herself, and that was it. The only way for that to happen was to make the offers so appealing that we could not resist. Then once she got us out to Malibu, she would find a way to get rid of Bob at any cost, so we could live together happily ever after.

Truth be told, I had known since the beginning that it was never going to work. I had told Bob hundreds of times that she was difficult and could be major trouble. However, Bob was so excited about his new career—and of course, I am always ready for a new adventure. I also tend to believe that everything happens for a reason, so I went along with it. Yet even the day before we were to leave Miami, I turned to Bob saying, "Let's not do it, we can still cancel everything and get out."

The situation really took a toll on Bob. He went into a major depression and apologized for pushing us to make this move. Even though the situation had caused a lot of chaos, I was relieved that I no longer had to deal with her craziness. All the drama was gone.

March 2009

Still, we had immediate issues to deal with. I went to the condominium office and explained the situation. They understood, and I was lucky that someone else was willing to rent my place. As I lay down in bed that night I thought *is that all there is?*

Peggy was my last link to the celebrity world. I thought about all those wonderful stars I worked with all these years. The fantastic life I had since that picture of me at four years old with my little velvet suit. I am so thankful that all those experiences happened to me. I have been so lucky and so grateful. One of my strengths is that I never miss or regret anything. Another chapter of my life is over; a door closed which means a window will open. I have Bob, my three girls, and life will go on.

What to do, where to go? Los Angeles? Nah, been there, done that. Miami? No, I could not think about going back when we had just left three months ago. I yawned, hoping that the answer would come soon. *If not, I'll think about it tomorrow. After all, tomorrow is another day.*

The End.

Top: 2013, with Bob; Bottom: with Benedicte and Fabrice at his daughter's wedding in 2010 (personal photos collection)

Top photo: with Bruno (L) and Guy, (R) 2010, the three musketeers in Brussels (personal photos collection); Bottom: 2018, 31 years later!

Acknowledgments

I would like to thank Marijke McCandless, Marni Freedman, Michael Polin, Mark Reichenthal, Addison Stonestreet, my mother-in-law, Carol Beelner, and my dear friend Pandora Van Buskirk for their help putting this book together.

Nadine, Guy, Bruno, Gregory, George, David and Alain, thanks for the wonderful memories.

To José Eber for taking a chance on me when nobody would.

To all my faithful clients, after all these years together.

To Fabrice and Benedicte, we might be thousands of miles apart but so close.

To Bob, my balance in life, to have stick with me all these years, aren't we a pair raggedy man?

Of course, all my girls, for their unconditional love.

Finally, my parents. Without them, maybe, I would not have experienced my adventurous life and be writing these words. Then again, one never knows ☺.

Celebrities

Cynthia Allison, Louis Aguirre, Patricia Arquette, Ann-Margret, Maud Adams, Annette Bening, Candice Bergen, Cindy Crawford, Cher, Dixie Carter, Stewart Copeland, Joana Carson, Claire Danes, Janice Dickinson, Joy Enriquez, Peter Frampton, Farrah Fawcett, Cornelia Guest, Linda Gray, Leeza Gibbons, Rachel Hunter, Woody Harellson, Lisa Hartman, Fawn Hall , Kathy Ireland, Don Johnson, Steve Kmetco, Sally Kellerman, Bette Midler, Ali McGraw, Victoria McMahon, Marilyn McCoo, Cathy Moriarty, Stevie Nicks, Sarah Purcell, Victoria Principal, Paloma Picasso, Linda Ronstadt, Jessica Simpson, Alicia Silverstone, Jaclyn Smith, Alana Stewart, Gene Simons, Shannon Tweed, Tracy Tweed, Elizabeth Taylor, Joan van Ark, Brenda Vaccaro, Vendella, Sylvie Vartan, Alexandra Von Furstenberg, Pia Zadora.

Periodicals

Allure, Vogue, Vogue Espana, W, Harper's Bazaar, Elle, In Style, Los Angeles Magazine, LA Times, American Salon, Miami's Herald, Entertainment Weekly, Woman's World, TV guide, Star, Holla!, Life, People, Ladies' Home Journal, S Florida magazine, Ocean Drive, El Nuevo Herald, Nuestra Gente, Modern Salon, Miami Mensual, Sophisticate's hairstyle guide, Indulge Magazine, Nous Deux, Good Housekeeping, Tribeza, Austin Home & Living, Great Looks Magazine, Beverly hills 213H Ultra, D magazine, Dallas Morning News, Dallas Time Herald, Lifestyle of the Rich and Famous.

Back cover photo credit Doug Gates

PS: Any photographers left without or wrong credits please contact me via email, so I can add your names in it.

Thank you

Made in the USA
Las Vegas, NV
06 June 2023

73033840R00148